WILD FL

AND WHERE TO FIND THEM
IN NORTHERN ENGLAND

VOLUME ONE

Northern Limestone

WILD FLOWERS
AND WHERE TO FIND THEM
IN NORTHERN ENGLAND

VOLUME ONE
Northern Limestone

LAURIE FALLOWS

FRANCES LINCOLN

A pocket guide to the wild flowers of Northern England, their historical, folk-mythological and medicinal attributes, with some background essays on related topics ✸ When and where to find them, their identifying features and flowering periods ✸ Detailed self-guided walks with simple maps to facilitate discovery

Volume 1
Northern Limestone
Limestone meadows, pastures and woods

Also in this series
Volume 2
Waterside Ways
Streamsides, pond margins, bog and coastal areas

Volume 3
Acid Uplands
Mountain, moorland and acid heaths

Frances Lincoln Ltd
4 Torriano Mews
Torriano Avenue
London NW5 2RZ
www.franceslincoln.com

© 2004 Laurie Fallows
Edited and designed by Jane Havell

ISBN 0 7112 2030 1

Origination by Imagescan, Malaysia
Printed in China by C S Graphics

Half-title page: (top) Mountain Pansy; (centre) Snowdrop; (bottom) Fragrant Orchid
Title pages: meadow of Rock Roses at Arnside (see Walk 7)

CONTENTS

Acknowledgements

I would like to express my heartfelt thanks to my wife Hazel, for her patience, support and understanding; to my daughter Jane and grandson Andrew for their invaluable assistance in the hitherto dark realms of computer wizardry; to my other daughter Gay and friend Joyce Langtree for assistance with fieldwork and walk-planning; and to Gill Brook for 13 flower pictures, especially some rare orchids.

I would like to dedicate these three volumes to my late mother Mary, née Vickers, for stimulating my initial interest in the flowers that played such an important part in her life, especially in her native Corbridge on Tyne, Northumberland.

LF
Windermere
2003

INTRODUCTION

For over fifty years I have conducted guided walks for National Park and local government authorities, and for educational and recreational organisations in the Yorkshire Dales, the Lake District, the Cheviots, the Galloway Hills of southern Scotland, and Snowdonia. I have introduced many thousands of adults and occasionally schoolchildren to the countryside, stressing not only the physical enjoyment of the great outdoors but also an understanding of its scenery, its history and its wildlife.

The information most frequently requested concerned the identification, the habitats, the folklore, the culinary and medicinal uses of plants, and simple field guides to help with their recognition. As more and more people take quiet recreation in country walks, the need for simple, descriptive, illustrated guides to wild flowers has increased. Existing flower guides have a number of drawbacks for beginners. They often rely on a knowledge of botanical terms, and do not indicate where particular species may be found. Furthermore, most of those that give flowering periods relate to central and southern England, whereas in the north of the country the climate, altitude and latitude often delay flowering by several weeks.

The plants covered in these books are of course not specific to the region, but can be found in other regions with similar soils and climates throughout the rest of Britain and Europe, making these guides of universal value.

Descriptions are stated in the simplest terms, and do not require any knowledge of the technical vocabulary of botanists. Read in association with the colour photographs, they should prevent confusion and make for certain identification. The flowering charts are based on regular personal observation throughout the year, and should provide an accurate record of when to see the plants in flower in northern England.

The walks are located in the Lake District and Southern Lakeland, the Yorkshire Dales, and Upper Teesdale. The straightforward instructions are

Dalehead Farm and Pen-y-Ghent

illustrated by specially drawn, simple maps, with a note of the relevant Ordnance Survey maps for those who want further cartographical information. Distances are given in kilometres, miles and average times. While some of the walks are longer than others, the maps often show how they may be shortened. Occasionally, fairly steep gradients and rough or boggy terrain will be encountered – where appropriate, these factors are mentioned.

RESPECT FOR HABITATS

All the plants featured in this book have been recorded within two metres of public or permissive footpaths. If the walk guides are followed, there is no risk of trespass. Remember to tread carefully and avoid trampling plants when looking at or photographing them, especially rare species.

Plants must never be picked or uprooted. Apart from being illegal (see box, page 9), removing them detracts from the natural environment.

WILD PLANTS AND THE LAW

All plants growing in the wild and their habitats are protected by the Wildlife and Countryside Act, 1981. Section 13 states: 'It is an offence for anyone to intentionally pick, uproot or destroy any wild plant on schedule 8,' which includes, among others, Spring Gentians, Bluebells, Pennyroyal, Teesdale Sandwort, Slender Naiad and some ferns, lichens and mosses. European legislation embodied in Conservation (Natural Habitats, etc.) Regulations 1994 adds further plants including Lady's Slipper Orchid, Shore Dock and Yellow Marsh Saxifrage. Section 13 (1)(b) of the 1981 Act states: 'it is an offence for any unauthorised person to intentionally uproot *any* wild plant,' – i.e., whether it is protected or not. Dealing in wild plants is forbidden under Section13 (2) (9a), which makes it an offence to 'sell, offer or expose for sale or possess or transport for the purpose of sale, or advertisement of intent to sell, any live or dead wild plant (or any part of or anything derived from such a plant) on schedule 8.'

Section 4 (3) of the Theft Act 1968 states that the picking of wild flowers, fruit or fungi for reward is considered to be theft. Uprooting a whole plant may also be considered theft. In Scotland, damage to flowers or plants on someone's property may be punishable as vandalism under the Criminal Law (Consolidation) (Scotland) Act 1995, Section 52, or as the common law crime of malicious mischief.

CONSUMPTION

The herbal uses described in this guide are for general interest only. Plants and plant extracts must not be applied to the skin or taken internally without reference to a qualified herbalist or at least an up-to-date herbal. Very careful identification is essential before any kind of experiment. Even in recent times, people have died through incorrect identification of plants – for example, by confusing Foxglove leaves with Comfrey. Identification should be by examining the whole plant, not just the flower or the leaf alone, since there are many superficial similarities.

HOW TO USE THE
FLOWER DIRECTORY

The plants are grouped according to the main colours of their flowers. However, many may be present in different colours – for example, Mountain Pansies are normally yellow in the Dales, but more likely to be blue or purple in Teesdale; Milkwort varies from blue or pink to white. Flower colour should be only one factor in identifying a species.

CHARTS

The Directory is preceded by colour charts, showing the months in which the plants may be seen in flower in northern England. Colours can vary considerably, even within species, so this should be taken as only a rough guide to aid identification. For simplification, and because colour is often subjective, the charts include some flowers that fit only marginally into the given colour categories.

While the charts are a general guide to flowering times in Northern England, individual specimens may flower outside these months. This may be because of peculiar local conditions, or because some species flower in profusion for a month or two and then produce a second flush later in the year. Groundsel, Chickweed and Red Campion may be seen virtually all the year round.

The charts are original, and have been compiled over six years by personal observation throughout the year. Flowering times may therefore vary from those published in other guides, many of which describe lower latitudes and altitudes. However, the region does range from the mild, moist southern Lakeland through the drier and higher Yorkshire Dales to the wet high altitude of Upper Teesdale, so variation is inevitable.

PHOTOGRAPHS

Each species is illustrated by a colour photograph, showing the general appearance of the plant, and the shape and relative size of its leaves and flowers. Please note that the scale of the individual photographs is not consistent.

NAMES

The main regional vernacular name is given first, then any other names in common use. Where there are many alternative names, only a selection is given. Vernacular names can be confusing. In different parts of the country, a single flower can have many different names – Cuckoo Pint, for example, has at least ninety recorded local names. The name Thunderflower is used for both Wood Anemone and Wood Cranesbill; Aaron's Rod for Agrimony and Great Mullein. The Bluebell of England becomes the Hyacinth in parts of Scotland, and their Bluebell is the English Harebell. Latin names are therefore also given to aid precise identification. Wherever possible, the origin and explanation of both Latin and common names are also expounded.

ABBREVIATIONS

aka	also known as
Arab	Arabic
AS	Anglo-Saxon
Celt	Celtic
Fr	French
Ger	German
Gk	Greek
L	Latin
ODan	Old Danish
OE	Old English
OFr	Old French
ON	Old Norse

HEIGHT AND FLOWERING MONTHS

When identifying a plant do not refer just to the photograph, but also to the height in the written description.

DESCRIPTION

The first paragraph describes general characteristics. The second paragraph gives particulars of where the plant grows, and an indication of its place in folklore and in folk and contemporary medicine.

IDENTIFICATION TIPS

When trying to identify a plant you do not know, it is important to consider all its features – particularly the shape of both flower and leaves, whether or

BOTANICAL TERMS

Every effort has been made to keep plant descriptions as simple as possible, but a few botanical terms are unavoidable.

alternate arranged alternately up the stem

annual completing a full life cycle in one year

anthers cases on top of stamens that contain pollen

basal just above ground level at the foot of the stem

biennial forming a rosette of basal leaves the first year; raising a stem, flowering and dying in the second year

bract small, leaf-like organ on flower stem

calyx sepals at flower base, often joined in a cup or tube

deciduous shedding leaves in the autumn

floret individual flower in a tight arrangement, as in Daisy

labiate in two parts, like lips

lanceolate lance-shaped

leaflet one division of a compound leaf

lobed divided into sections

node place on stem where leaves arise

ovary the seed container below the style

perennial going on year after year with incremental vegetative increase

persistent leaves overwinter on plant

petals inner leaves, often highly coloured, of flower heads

pinnate divided into leaflets either side of stalk

raceme flower spike

rhizome swollen underground root that feeds the plant

sepals outer leaves of flower buds and holders of flower

stamens male pollen-bearing organs

stigma top of the style that receives the pollen

stipules small leaf-like appendages at the base of leaf stalks

stolons creeping stems that produce new plant stems at intervals

style tube or stalk between stigma and ovary

trefoil with three leaflets, as in Clover

tubers swollen underground organs with plant food

wintergreen retaining old leaves over winter

not parts are hairy, whether it is growing in dry or wet conditions, in sun or in shade, and whether it is shunned or devoured by livestock. Consider its situation in relation to the type of ground it is growing in and its association with other plant life. Climate and altitude can also cause considerable variation. The walks section gives further information about when and where to locate certain species.

A small hand lens of 10× magnification is very helpful in identification, and also reveals the hidden beauties of diminutive species.

PLANTS AS MEDICINES

Plants have held the interest of man far back into the mists of time. Apart from their beauty, perfumes, and value as food and flavourings, their intrinsic medicinal properties have been the source of continuous research and experimentation. Folk remedies, linked with superstition and magic and built up by hard and often fatal experience, have been passed on by oral tradition through witchdoctors and local healers even to the present day. No doubt some of their beliefs and practices were adopted by the educated clerks and philosophers whose studies and experiments classified, systematised and recorded contemporary knowledge.

The earliest record of plants used as medicines was found in a 60,000-year-old burial site in Iraq. No other very early records survive, but from about 1500 BC herbal lore, often with associated spells, incantations and rituals, appeared in Egypt and India.

CLASSICAL TIMES

In the fourth century BC the Greek physician Hippocrates ridiculed belief in the supernatural attributes of plants, claiming that all illnesses were natural, often related to environmental factors, and required natural remedies. Based on the belief that the world was made up of **four elements** – fire, air, earth and water – he suggested that the body was made up of **four humours**: blood, yellow bile, black bile and phlegm. Disease, he claimed, was the result of imbalance in these fluids. He also attributed to plants **four properties** – hot, dry, cold and moist – which could be applied to restore balance, and physical and mental health.

In the third century BC, Theophrastus of Lesbos produced treatises on plant classification and outlined some four hundred simple remedies. These were incorporated by Pliny the Elder in his 37-volume *Naturalis Historia* of

77 AD. At about the same time, Pedanius Dioscorides, a Greek physician to the Roman army, produced details of about five hundred medicinal plants drawn from earlier Greek, Arabian and Egyptian sources.

During the second century AD, Galen, the physician from Asia Minor and friend of the Emperor Marcus Aurelius, extended Hippocrates' theory of the four humours by suggesting that these were reflected in **four temperaments**: sanguine or buoyant, choleric or quick-tempered, melancholic or dejected, and phlegmatic or sluggish. He averred that physical and mental balance could be restored by the application of the opposite properties – for example, the hot, dry symptoms of a fever could be assuaged by the use of herbs that were cool and moist. Purging and bloodletting were also used, often with dire or fatal consequences.

KEY: Elements Humours Properties Temperaments

These theories, disseminated throughout the widespread Roman Empire, were almost universally adopted in the west. They tended to inhibit medical advance for many centuries, since they distracted from an understanding of the true nature of disease.

THE DARK AGES

Following the defeat and dissolution of the Roman Empire, there was little advance in medical thinking apart from in a few monastic institutions, but academic writings were scarce. There was a local drift back to oral folk traditions, closely allied with superstition and magic. The extensive trade in herbs and spices almost disappeared in northern Europe, though it still prospered in some Mediterranean countries and in the east.

The Persian physician Avicenna (AD 979–1037) made a significant advance in herbal therapy by discovering how to distil volatile oils from plants and flowers. With the rise of Islam and the extensive Ottoman Empire, classical thinking and practice which had been preserved and elaborated in the Arabic culture spread back through North Africa to Italy, Spain and Portugal, where medical schools were founded. In the eleventh century, Constantinus Africanus and Gerard of Cremona translated Arabic texts on medicine into Latin, making them accessible to European monasteries, most of which had a rule of caring for the sick.

THE MIDDLE AGES

The Norman invasion of 1066 gave further stimulus to medical thought and practice in Britain. New herbs were brought in and cultivated to treat ailments and illnesses, and the use of herbs and spices in cooking was introduced. Precious manuscripts describing the properties and uses of indigenous plants were brought over. In 1317, the Englishman John Gaddesden wrote *Rosa Medicinae*, a comprehensive picture of contemporary medical practice.

Up to this date all writings had been in Latin. However, by the end of the fourteenth century a number of vernacular texts had appeared which further disseminated medical thinking. The prevalent plagues and pestilences failed to stimulate investigation or research, since they were put down to Acts of God. But diet and exercise were advocated, and people were advised to avoid hot baths and sleeping after meals, and to ensure that their homes were filled with the perfume of violets, bay leaves, fennel, mint, roses and other aromatics.

THE RENAISSANCE

Towards the end of the fifteenth century, the invention of the printing press facilitated the large-scale reproduction and distribution of texts. The rising number of universities brought together scholars from a wide field, concentrating like minds in research and debate. Medicine and botany were closely associated.

In the early sixteenth century, the Swiss doctor Theophrastus Bombast von Hohenheim, known as Paracelsus, a professor at Basle University, revived and gave academic respectability to an old folk medicine hypothesis that he called the Doctrine of Signatures. He claimed that every plant was 'signed' in some aspect of colour, shape or design to show which illness or condition it would cure. For example, St John's Wort, with its translucent, pore-like dots on the leaves and blood-red juice, would heal flesh wounds; Eyebright, with a flower the throat of which resembles a bloodshot eye, would be the choice for eye complaints; and the speckled leaves of Lung-wort, resembling human lungs, was a favourite for chest conditions. This theory was relatively shortlived in academic circles, but persisted for centuries in folk medicine.

ENGLISH NOTABLES

In 1551, William Turner, a physician and naturalist who was the son of a Northumbrian tanner, published *A New Herbal*, which strongly influenced his peers and earned him the title of Father of English Botany. Even more popular was *The English Physitian* of 1562 by the astrologer and botanist Nicholas Culpeper. He suggested that all plants were influenced by the planets and the signs of the zodiac. For example, of Orchids he wrote: 'they are hot and moist in operation, under the domination of Venus, and provoke lust, while the dried and withered roots restrain.' His theory was accepted for only a short time, but his remedies were influential for many years. In 1597 John Gerard of Nantwich published his *Historie of Plants*, largely plagiarised from European herbalists but emphasising a plantsman's viewpoint, and advising remedies that were widely followed.

From all over Europe, plant expeditions were being mounted by botanists, often ship's doctors, who brought back exotic plants to be grown in botanical gardens alongside indigenous species, so that their growth and medicinal uses could be studied. Among the foremost English botanists was John Ray (1628–1705), a great collector and grower who made a significant contribution to the classification of plants. He influenced the Swedish scholar Carl Linnaeus, whose *Plantara* of 1753 and 1754 set out the system which is now universally used (this is described in Volume 2, *Waterside Ways*).

ORTHODOX MEDICINE

During the late seventeenth century, the study of medicine and of botany began to separate, herbals being replaced by 'pharmacopoeias' for doctors, and 'floras' for botanists. At the beginning of the twentieth century, most of the remedies used in orthodox medicine were still plant-based, but gradually synthetic chemicals came to replace the plant macerations and infusions, a process that was encouraged by the pharmaceutical companies. Essential chemicals are still extracted from one or two plants, such as digitoxin from the Foxglove, but aspirin, once based on extracts from Meadowsweet and Willow, can now be produced synthetically. This helps the conservation of wild plants. Nevertheless, scientists at one leading British pharmaceutical company alone still analyse an amazing thirty thousand plant chemicals a week in search of useful components.

COMPLEMENTARY MEDICINE

Homeopathy, once proscribed, has seen a resurgence in Britain. It is based on natural plant extracts, administered in combinations in greatly diluted quantities. Dr Edward Bach, a London practitioner, developed a series of flower remedies using plants such as Agrimony, Centaury, Ling and Rock Rose with pure water and a few drops of brandy to treat various emotional states and associated problems.

A French chemist, Professor René-Maurice Gattefoss, made use of essential oils in treating wounded soldiers during the First World War. He found that some oils, particularly lavender, helped to detoxify the body when wounds had become infected, a practice he named Aromatherapy. His student Madame Maury developed his theories by using plant essences in skin care and massage. New approaches are still being pursued in many different directions.

GEOLOGY OF THE REGION

Plant life varies in any region by virtue of the soil, the altitude, the climate and, over the past ten thousand years, the impact of man and his farming activities. In general terms, with the exception of lower areas blanketed by river-borne silts or glacial deposits, or wet uplands carpeted by peat, soils tend to reflect the underlying rocks from which they derive. It is not relevant to this brief survey to discuss the origins and development of the very oldest volcanic rocks in the region. Suffice it to say that they form the crust of the earth on which were superimposed newer rocks created by the deposition of their eroded silts and sands or animal remains, and by volcanic intrusions.

ORDOVICIAN PERIOD

Most of the superstructure of the area was developed between five hundred and three hundred million years ago, when the imperceptibly moving crustal plate on which it stands lay under a great ocean surrounded by land masses south of the Tropic of Capricorn. Rapid erosion of the mountains poured mud and silt into this vast marine basin. Over the millennia the detritus built up to a considerable depth, and was consolidated into the mudstones and siltstones that we now refer to as the **Skiddaw Slates**. The rolling hills they formed contrast dramatically with the rugged volcanic crags to their south, the **Borrowdale Volcanics**. The sheer weight of great depths of mud and silt, coupled with the convergence of crustal plates, created violent earth movements and intense volcanic activity. This generated lava deposits and showered deep layers of volcanic ash over the older rocks on the surface, and intruded molten magma below the surface, which then cooled into granite.

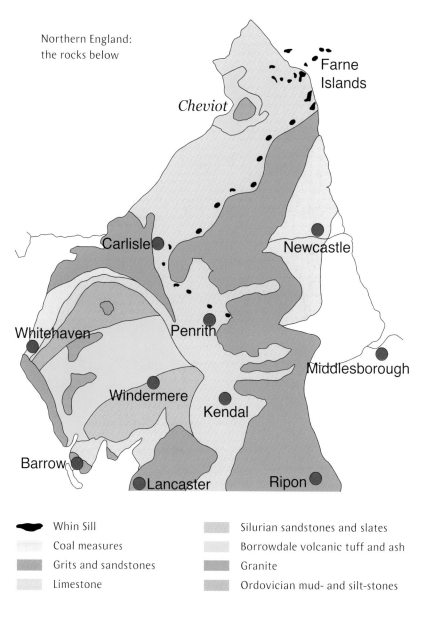

Northern England:
the rocks below

Farne
Islands

Cheviot

Carlisle

Newcastle

Whitehaven

Penrith

Middlesborough

Windermere

Kendal

Barrow

Lancaster

Ripon

Whin Sill	Silurian sandstones and slates
Coal measures	Borrowdale volcanic tuff and ash
Grits and sandstones	Granite
Limestone	Ordovician mud- and silt-stones

SILURIAN PERIOD

Eventually the south of the area subsided, and a further period of submarine development took place. Newer volcanic rocks rapidly eroded, and spewed silt and sand into the sea to build up the shales and sandstones of the **Windermere Silurian rocks**. Like the Skiddaw group, these are roundly undulating in profile.

Some forty million years on, deep-rooted disturbances in the molten rocks beneath the earth's surface pushed up the **mountains of the Lake District, the Pennines**, and large areas of **Scotland**. In places like **Shap, Eskdale** and **Cheviot**, granite broke through to the surface as volcanoes. Simultaneously, sideways pressure folded the surrounding sedimentary rocks into large-scale corrugations, sometimes forcing horizontal layers into vertical formation. This is known as the **Caledonian Uplift**.

CARBONIFEROUS PERIOD

There followed a period of erosion that tended to level off the folds at the surface, before the area round the central Lakeland core subsided to a little below sea level. By now, the continental slab had edged into the tropics and in shallow, clear lagoons the coastal water spawned myriads of shellfish and

GEOLOGICAL TIME CHART

Period	million yrs ago	Location	Origin
Carboniferous			
Whin Sill	295	Under N Pennines	Volcanic
Millstone Grit	300	Central Pennines	Deltaic
Coal Measures	310	W Cumberland, Durham and Northumberland	Swamp
Yoredale Series		Yorkshire Dales	Cyclic deposition
Great Limestone	345	S and E of Lakes	Marine skeletons
Caledonian Uplift	410	Lakes and Pennines	Volcanic
Silurian	450	South Lakes	Deep ocean silt
Borrowdale Volcanics	460	Central Lakes	Volcanic
Ordovician	510	North Lakes	Deep sea mud

Arctic conditions across Whernside and Ingleborough from Lovely Seat

corals. As they died and fell to the bottom among the fine silts, they built up a lime-rich mud that consolidated over time into solid limestone up to 1,500 metres thick.

Later in the period, often under its own accruing weight, the sea bed fell, then built up again, changing the nature of the sediments. From lime-rich marine life to fine silt, then sand, the process repeated itself several times. This created the **Yoredale Series**, named after the valley of the River Ure where it is so graphically illustrated. Eventually, the sea bed built up to the surface where, in lush swamps, primitive ferns and trees grew and died to form layers of coal-bearing rocks. This Carboniferous period occupied the second fifty million years after the Caledonian Uplift.

As the swamps eventually gave way to sandy deltas, coarse sands bearing rounded pebbles of white quartz built up, layer upon layer, to form the dark, familiar **Millstone Grit** that caps the Pennines, in particular on the summits of **Whernside**, **Ingleborough**, **Pen-y-Ghent** and **Great Whernside**.

Around 295 million years ago, the grand finale of this dramatic rock production occurred in the form of a massive intrusion of molten magma into the upper Carboniferous levels. The result of this, the **Hercynian Uplift**, was the great **Whin Sill**, molten quartz-dolerite that crystallised into a sheet up to 30 metres thick, extending nearly 5,000 square kilometres under the whole of Northern England. It is exposed spectacularly in the **Farne Islands**, along the **Roman Wall**, down the **Eden Valley** especially at **High Cup Nick**, and at **High Force** and **Cauldron Snout** in **upper Teesdale**. It had the effect of roasting the limestone with which it made contact into the 'sugar-lime-stone' that nurtures some of upper Teesdale's rarest plants.

Apart from surface and coastal erosion, minor earthquakes and occasional subsidence, the area suffered little structural change for the next 294 million years, although the dipping eastern fringe was inundated and deposited with marine debris.

THE ICE AGES

A mere million years ago, a severe climatic change swathed most of the land in deep snow. Consolidated by their own weight into ice, vast glaciers eased downwards to the seas, plucking stone from the sides of the now U-shaped valleys. As they carved through the Dales, they carried away the exposed shales and sandstones, leaving the more resistant limestones prominent as cliffs (scars) staircasing up the valley sides, a feature that predominates in **upper Wensleydale**, **Wharfedale** and **Swaledale**.

In places, softer rocks and soils were scoured off the limestone plateaux, exposing the water-worn surfaces we call **limestone pavement**. The acid nature of the rain percolating through weaknesses in the alkaline limestone dissolved some of it and created runnels (grykes), with blocks (clints) standing proud above them like stepping stones. The deep grykes, out of reach to sheep, can harbour delicate plant life. The glaciers deposited some of their accumulated debris in moraines and drumlins, and cloaked large areas with boulder clay. The ice finally began to melt only ten thousand years ago, and the melt waters carved new river channels with spectacular waterfalls, such as at **Malham Cove**.

Opposite: Cauldron Snout, showing the Whin Sill, formed during the Carboniferous period

Limestone pavement in South Cumbria

Eventually the frost, deep in the earth, also melted and allowed surface water to drain down through the limestone, leaving dry river channels on the surface (such as **Watlowes**, near Malham Cove) and creating streams, potholes and caves underground.

Opposite: hay meadow, Harrowside, Windermere

SOILS

In general terms, the older Ordovician and Silurian rocks, the volcanic rocks of the Lake District and the millstone grit capping the Yorkshire hills, produce heavy, often badly drained, acid soils. The sandstones and shales of the Yoredale series also degenerate into heavy, waterlogged acid soils, as seen on the flanks of the higher Dales peaks. On the boulder clays and impervious rocks at altitude, bogs develop.

On the other hand, the limestones of the Lakeland fringe and the Yorkshire Dales produce light, crumbly soils, rich in calcium that quickly breaks down plant and animal debris into valuable humus. Heavy rainfall can leach out the calcium, and farmers compensate for this by applying powdered lime to 'sweeten' their fields. Many lime kilns bear testimony to this practice. In the valley bottoms the accumulated alluvium, where drained, creates ideal soils for the flower-rich hay meadows for which the Dales are so famed.

BRITISH ORCHIDS

To many people, the word 'orchid' conjures up the exotic epiphytic species of the tropics or sub-tropics. They live on trees or rocks, not as parasites but obtaining nourishment from the atmosphere, from rainwater and from humus in bark crevices through specially adapted roots. They make up over half of the world's 750 genera and 2,000 species of orchid. The remainder, which include the 50 or so British orchids, are terrestrial or ground-growing plants.

The Latin name *Orchis* derives from the Greek for testicle, which their fleshy roots or tubers were thought to resemble. Their strap-like leaves support single, unbranched spikes of purple, pink, brown, white or green flowers. Each flower consists of three sepals above and three petals below. The central petal at the base is lobed, and enlarged to form a platform for pollinating insects. It is often extended backwards to form a balancing spur.

The reproductive organs are united into a single column with the pollen at the top just above the ovary. The pollen consists not of a powder but of a cluster of two, four, six or eight globular masses called pollinia. When nectar-seeking insects visit the plant, the pollinia are easily detached and transferred. They stick to the insects, which carry them away to pollinate other plants as their quest for nectar continues.

The seeds produced are so small that, unlike other plants, orchids have no inbuilt larder on which to develop. They enlist the aid of mycorhiza, a fungus common in most soils. Mycorhiza obtain their nourishment from humus in the soil, and some of this is passed on to the symbiotic orchid seedlings. Each seedling develops a small tuber or mycorhizome, which is eventually replaced by its own mature tuber.

This is a long slow process. It can take several years before the new plant can throw up leaves and a flower. Spotted Orchids may not flower for 4–5 years after germination, Butterfly Orchids for 5–8 years, Twayblades for 15 years. Thereafter orchids can flower for several more years, reproducing annually by vegetative means, with the exception of the Fragrant and Bee Orchids which put all their energy into flowering and producing seed, then die.

The Bird's Nest Orchid is one of only three saprophytic British orchids, the others being the rare Coral-Root found on North Walney Island, and the rarer Ghost Orchid not known in the north. Saprophytic plants, possessing little or no chlorophyll, cannot make their own food so they tap the rich humus of dead plant and animal matter on woodland floors (as opposed to parastic plants such as Broomrape, Toadstools and Dodders which get their sugars from other living plants).

This amazing life-cycle, as well as their flowers which are especially spectacular when seen en masse, makes the orchid a fascinating plant and worthy of protection. Within living memory we have virtually lost the Lady's Slipper Orchid from the wild, but it is now slowly being re-established in its former habitats, thanks to the Royal Horticultural Society's research staff at Kew Gardens who have produced seedlings by vegetative reproduction and donated them to certain wildlife trusts.

By preserving and respecting these plants within their environments, we can ensure that they will be appreciated and enjoyed by future generations.

FLOWER DIRECTORY

PLANTS IN FLOWER	Jan	Feb	Mar	Apr	May	June	July	Aug	Sep	Oct	Nov	Dec
Agrimony												
Bedstraw, Lady's												
Black Medick												
Cat's Ear												
Celandine, Lesser												
Cinquefoil, Creeping												
Cinquefoil, Shrubby												
Cowslip												
Crosswort												
Daffodil												
Dandelion												
Globe Flower												
Golden Rod												
Hawkweed, Mouse Ear												
Herb Bennet												
Lettuce, Wall												
Meadow Rue, Lesser												
Mullein, Great												
Orchid, Lady's Slipper												
Oxlip, False												
Pansy, Mountain												
Pepper, Wall												
Primrose												
Ragwort												
Rock-Rose												
Rock-Rose, Hoary												
Sage, Wood												
St John's Wort, Hairy												
Silverweed												
Spikenard, Ploughman's												
Thistle, Carline												
Tormentil												
Trefoil, Bird's Foot												

PLANTS IN FLOWER	Jan	Feb	Mar	Apr	May	June	July	Aug	Sep	Oct	Nov	Dec
Anemone, Wood												
Baneberry												
Bedstraw, Limestone												
Burnet, Saxifrage												
Daisy												
Daisy, Dog												
Dropwort												
Eyebright												
Flax, Fairy												
Gromwell												
Jack by the Hedge												
Lily of the Valley												
Meadowsweet												
Mountain Everlasting												
Nightshade, Enchanter's												
Orchid, Greater Butterfly												
Pennycress, Alpine												
Pignut												
Ramsons												
Sandwort, Spring												
Sanicle												
Saxifrage, Rue-Leaved												
Snowdrop												
Solomon's Seal, Angular												
Sorrel, Wood												
Strawberry, Barren												
Strawberry, Wild												
Sweet Cicely												
Traveller's Joy												
Whitlow Grass												
Whitlow Grass, Hoary												
Woodruff												

PLANTS IN FLOWER	Jan	Feb	Mar	Apr	May	June	July	Aug	Sep	Oct	Nov	Dec
Cuckoo Pint				■	■							
Hellebore, Stinking		■	■	■								
Herb Paris					■	■						
Lady's Mantle					■	■						
Mercury, Dog's				■	■							
Pellitory of the Wall						■	■	■	■	■		
Twayblade					■	■						

PLANTS IN FLOWER	Jan	Feb	Mar	Apr	May	June	July	Aug	Sep	Oct	Nov	Dec
Felwort							■	■	■			
Orchid, Early Purple				■	■							
Saxifrage, Purple			■	■								
Self Heal						■	■	■	■			
Thistle, Melancholy							■	■				
Thyme, Wild						■	■	■				

PLANTS IN FLOWER	Jan	Feb	Mar	Apr	May	June	July	Aug	Sep	Oct	Nov	Dec
Avens, Water				■	■	■						
Basil, Wild							■	■	■			
Betony						■	■	■	■			
Bistort					■	■	■	■				
Centaury							■	■	■			
Cranesbill, Cut-Leaved					■	■	■	■	■			
Cranesbill, Dove's Foot				■	■	■	■	■	■			
Cranesbill, Shining					■	■	■	■				
Herb Robert				■	■	■	■	■	■	■	■	
Milkmaid				■	■	■						
Orchid, Burnt-Tip					■	■						
Orchid, Early Marsh					■	■						
Orchid, Fragrant						■	■					
Orchid, Pyramidal						■	■	■				
Orchid, Spotted					■	■	■	■				
Primrose, Bird's Eye					■	■						
Squinancywort						■	■	■	■			
Toothwort			■	■	■							
Valerian						■	■	■				

PLANTS IN FLOWER	Jan	Feb	Mar	Apr	May	June	July	Aug	Sep	Oct	Nov	Dec
Agrimony, Hemp							■	■	■			
Burnet, Salad					■	■	■	■				
Cranesbill, Bloody						■	■	■				
Cranesbill, Wood						■	■	■				
Helleborine, Broad-Leaved							■	■				
Helleborine, Dark Red							■	■				

PLANTS IN FLOWER	Jan	Feb	Mar	Apr	May	June	July	Aug	Sep	Oct	Nov	Dec
Bellflower, Creeping							■	■	■			
Bluebell				■	■	■						
Bugle				■	■	■						
Columbine					■	■						
Gentian, Spring				■	■							
Harebell							■	■	■			
Ivy, Ground				■	■	■						
Milkwort					■	■	■	■				
Scabious, Small							■	■	■			
Speedwell, Germander				■	■	■						
Violet, Dog				■	■							

PLANTS IN FLOWER	Jan	Feb	Mar	Apr	May	June	July	Aug	Sep	Oct	Nov	Dec
Orchid, Bird's Nest					■	■						
Orchid, Fly					■	■						

FERNS IN LEAF	Jan	Feb	Mar	Apr	May	June	July	Aug	Sep	Oct	Nov	Dec
Fern, Buckler, Rigid							■	■	■			
Fern, Hart's Tongue							■	■	■			
Fern, Limestone							■	■	■			
Fern, Maidenhair					■	■	■	■				
Fern, Male	■	■	■					■	■			
Fern, Male, Golden	■	■	■									
Fern, Rusty-Back							■	■	■			
Moonwort						■	■	■				
Spleenwort, Green					■	■						
Spleenwort, Maidenhair					■	■	■					
Wall Rue							■	■	■			

AGRIMONY

FAIRY'S ROD, FAIRY WAND, AARON'S ROD

Height 30–60cm/12–24in ☀ June–September

Agrimonia eupatoria
Gk *agrimonia*, heals the eyes; *Eupatoria*, after
Mithridates Eupator VI, 1st century BC, who
introduced it as a medicine

Faintly perfumed perennial, with a woody
root, erect, round and roughish stems, seldom
branched. Pinnate leaves like ash, 3–6 main
leaflets with smaller ones between, downy
below, sharply toothed. Small yellow flowers,
5-petalled, widely spaced, make slim spike.
Fruits are small oval burs, hooked and
furrowed.
    Staunches bleeding, encourages blood
clotting. Used against gastroenteritis, gall and
liver disorders, kidney and bladder infections,
gout and bruised joints. Gerard says a
decoction of the leaves is 'good for them that
have naughty livers'. Taken in wine against
snake bites. Yields a yellow dye.

BEDSTRAW, LADY'S

CHEESE RENNET, MAIDEN'S HAIR

Height 15–60cm/6–24in ☀ July–October

Galium verum
Gk *gala*, milk; L *verum*, true

A sprawling perennial with rounded stems
having 4 lines of hairs. Dark green shiny
leaves, hairy below in whorls of 8–12 with
down-facing margins. Golden flowers in a
fluffy oval bunch, smelling of honey. Small
green fruits turn black when ripe.
    Medieval lore had it that Mary lay on this
herb because the donkeys had eaten all the
hay, hence it was believed to bring safe and
easy childbirth. When dry, smells of new-
mown hay. Once used to stuff mattresses, as
it was believed to deter fleas. Used internally
against dropsy, kidney and bladder disorders
and stomach upsets, externally for skin
infections and slow-healing cuts and grazes.
In Northern England used as rennet in cheese-
making. Leaves yield yellow dye, roots red.

BLACK MEDICK

HOP MEDICK

Height 5–50cm/2–20in ❀ May–September

Medicago lupulina
L *medicago*, plant of the Medes;
lupulina, hop-like

A low prostrate downy annual with toothed
trefoil leaves with 2 leaf-like stipules at the
stem. Its tiny globe-shaped flowerheads have
10–50 separate florets. Fruits are little kidney-
shaped pods that blacken when ripe. Grows
in short grassland, preferably lime-rich.

Medicago was named by the Romans after
the fodder plant Lucerne, a close relative of
Black Medick. It superficially resembles Hop
Trefoil (*Trifolium campestre*, Vol. 2), which is
distinguished by its hop-like fruits when ripe.
Still grown as a fodder crop in many Eastern
European countries. One of a number of
trefoil plants worn in Ireland as Shamrock
on St Patrick's Day.

CAT'S EAR

Height 20–60cm/8–24in ❀ June–October

Hypochoeris radicata
Gk *hypo*, below; *choiros*, pig; L *radicata*, having
roots (all leaves rise direct from root)

A perennial with a long white unbranched tap
root that exudes white sap. Hairy leaves with
wavy toothed edges similar to Dandelion in
basal rosette. Erect, sparingly branched solid
stems have small dark scale-like bracts (cat's
ears) but no leaves. Solitary or few branched
flowers like slender Dandelions 2.5cm/1in
across. Fruits are orange in colour with
parachutes.

It is often rooted up by pigs, hence its
botanical name. Uses are limited, but it can
act as a winter salad plant.

The Spotted Cat's Ear (found, for example,
on Humphrey Head) is similar, but its leaves
are strongly toothed and spotted purplish
black. Flowers on both species usually solitary.

CELANDINE, LESSER

PILEWORT, FOALFOOT, SPRING MESSENGER,
GOLDEN GUINEA

Height 6–15cm/2¹/₂–6in ✿ **March–May**

Ranunculus ficaria
L *rana*, frog (grows in wet places);
ficus, fig-shaped (tubers)

A low hairless perennial with knobbly
tuberous roots like piles. Fleshy dark-green
leaves, long-stalked, heart-shaped, sometimes
with dark blotches. Solitary flowers with 8–2
glossy yellow petals that close in dull weather.
Fruits in a small round cluster.

   Formerly the leaves were used medicinally
against piles and scurvy. Cosmetic lotion made
from Celandine cleanses skin, closes pores
and removes wrinkles. Use leaves sparingly
in salads or sandwiches; leaves, stalks and buds
as spinach; buds can be preserved like capers.
The name Celandine comes from Greek for
a swallow, a bird believed to use the flowers
to improve the sight of its chicks.

CINQUEFOIL, CREEPING

Height 5–10cm/2–4in ✿ **June–September**

Potentilla reptans
L *potens*, powerful; *reptans*, prostrate

A perennial rising from a stout stock of
creeping stems (up to 100cm/40 in) that root
at nodes. Toothed leaves are divided into 5 or
7 leaflets (like Horse Chestnut) on long stalks.
Single 5-petalled flowers on long slim stalks
from leaf nodes. Yellow petals notched. Fruit
a dry achene (like a small nut).

   Dioscorides said this plant, called 'Five
Fingers', was good against malaria, based on
its magical powers, but Gerard dismissed this
as 'foolish'. Astringent roots and leaves used
as a febrifuge, mouthwash, and against
haemorrhages and dysentery; also for bathing
cuts and for piles. Roots once used for tanning.
In Scotland it was hung in doorways to deter
witches.

CINQUEFOIL, SHRUBBY

Height 45–90cm/18–36in   ❀ May–July

Potentilla fruticosa
L *potens*, powerful (healer); *fruticosa*, shrubby

A deciduous shrub with small hairy grey leaves
having 5 slender leaflets borne on grey hairy
stalks supported by woody stems. Single or
small groups of hairy calices hold 2cm/¼in
yellow flowers, each with 5 rounded
unnotched petals. Male and female flowers
on separate plants. Seeds quite freely. Prefers
a damp lime-rich rocky habitat, and is often
found at riversides or on islands. A true relict
species of the Ice Age, it is a rare plant of
Upper Teesdale and the Lake District, also
of the Burren in Galway. It is widespread,
occurring in northern areas from Europe to
the Himalayas.

Cultivated species of different colours are
used in gardens and parks.

COWSLIP

PAIGLE, PETERKEYS, PALSYWORT,
COWSTRIPLINGS

Height 10–30cm/4–12in   ❀ April–June

Primula veris
L *primus*, first; *veris*, spring

Delicately perfumed perennial with a rosette
of hairy wrinkled toothed leaves, sharply
narrowed near the stalk like a short-handled
spoon. Flowers in clusters usually drooping to
one side, each on a leafless stalk. A pale green
calyx supports a yellow flower with an orange
centre. Seed pods persist for a long time.

Wide medicinal uses, including as diuretic;
expectorant; for rheumatism and gout; coughs,
colds, flu and bronchitis; catarrh and kidney
complaints; insomnia and migraine, and to
cure 'vertigo, false apparitions, phrenzies,
falling sickness, palsies, convulsions, cramps
and nerve pains'. Leaves and flowers used in
salads, as pot herbs, and in puddings and tarts.

CROSSWORT

HONEYWORT

Height 22–38cm/9–15in April–July

Galium cruciata
Gk *gala*, milk (continental species *Galium verum* used as rennet); *cruciata*, cross-shaped (leaves)

A member of the Bedstraw family. A soft hairy perennial with a creeping rootstock. Erect square stems have whorls of 4 elliptical leaves spaced upwards like crosses, with clusters of small yellow flowers in the angles between leaves and stem. Honey-scented. Fruits like minute black cherries on long stalks.

A strewing herb to sweeten stone floors. Roots yield a red dye. Recommended by Gerard for healing wounds because of its 'signature' of the cross, and to be taken in wine against ruptures. The suffix '-wort' indicates culinary or medicinal use.

DAFFODIL

LENT LILY

Height 36cm/14in March–May

Narcissus pseudonarcissus
Gk, name of god turned into this plant after his suicide; *pseudo*, false or bastard
Daffodil from Dutch *de affodil*, from Fr *afrodille*, from L *asphodelus* (its former classification)

A bulbous perennial that often grows in small clumps. A sheath of blue-green lance-like leaves clasps a flattened hollow stem that bears a single horizontal or nodding flower: a large trumpet with a flared end and a whorl of 6 paler yellow sepals. A papery brown spathe protects the young bud and hangs down over the seed case which develops into 3 chambers.

Used as a purgative, an emetic and a cure for erysipalis and palsy. Said to bloom on St David's Day, it is the national symbol of Wales. National Daffodil Day celebrated by Marie Curie Cancer Relief as the symbol of new hope and life.

DANDELION

PISSABED, DEVIL'S MILK PAIL, HEART FEVER GRASS

Height 5–30cm/2–12in ❀ February–October

Taraxacum officinalis
L *Taraxacum*, from Persian name for bitter herb;
officinalis, from *opificina*, monastic herb store
Dandelion from Fr *Dent-de-Lion*

A robust perennial rising from a long carrot-like
tap root. Soft fleshy leaves form a rosette at
base, deeply toothed. Hollow rubbery stems full
of white sap support single flowers that close at
night or on dull days. Each head has up to 200
closely packed florets that develop into the
familiar Dandelion clock, with seeds on fine
parachutes.

   Dandelion wine good for indigestion or
kidney troubles. Milky sap cures warts. A
diuretic, used for dyspepsia. Leaves are used for
soup, or cooked with butter, lemon and cider
vinegar as a vegetable. Buds pickled in vinegar
used like capers. Dried, ground and roasted roots
make a caffeine-free alternative to coffee.

GLOBE FLOWER

DOUBLE DUMPLINGS (TEESDALE),
LOCKER GOWANS

Height 30–60cm/12–24in ❀ May–August

Trollius europaeus
L *europaeus*, european
Globe Flower from Swiss-German *Trollblum*

A hairless shiny perennial with deeply cut,
hand-shaped leaves similar to Meadow
Cranesbill, but not downy. An upright,
branched stem bears singly yellow globes
comprising about 10 incurved sepals (no
petals). Fruits are a cluster of dry seed cases as
with Columbines. Likes damp rich meadows
in hilly districts. Grows in Northern Britain
mainly on limestone, and from the Alps
northwards across to Siberia.

   First recorded in Northern England in
1597 by Gerard, but without reference to any
herbal use. Any potentially useful medicinal
properties would be lost in drying or heating.
Cultivated as a garden plant.

GOLDEN ROD

AARON'S ROD, FAREWELL SUMMER

Height 5–60cm/2–24in ❀ July–October

Solidago virgaurea
L *solidago*, to make whole or heal;
virgaurea, a golden rod

Stout upright perennial with erect downy
stems, sometimes branched at top. Leaves
toothed, upper lance-shaped, unstalked;
lower stalked and wider in middle. Flowers on
branched spikes, short-stalked, yellow, shortly
rayed with narrow sepal-like bract. Brown
seeds have parachutes of white hairs.

Much used as an ointment or hot potion
in the 16th century to heal wounds from duels
or stabbings. Recommended by herbalists for
kidney ailments and mouth ulcers. Used in
proprietary medicines for urinary problems,
arthritis and rheumatism. Also once used for
bronchitis and tuberculosis. Tea made from
the leaves aids digestion. Helpful in cases of
diphtheria.

HAWKWEED, MOUSE EAR

Height 5–30cm/2–12in ❀ May–October

Hieracium pilosella
Gk *hieracium*, hawk; L *pilosus*, long-haired

A hairy perennial rising from a long slender
creeping rhizome producing many rooting
stems. Rosettes of pale green elliptical leaves,
hairy above and whitish below. Single flower
heads on leafless stems, light yellow with outer
petals reddish below. Fruits a cluster of tiny
parachutes.

The Greeks believed that hawks ate the
milky sap to improve their eyesight. A mildly
astringent, anti-inflammatory diuretic that
stimulates bile flow. An infusion of the whole
herb, fresh or dried, is taken internally for
enteritis, pyelitis, cystitis and flu, or on cotton
wool as a plug for nose-bleeds. Also used
externally as a compress or for bathing cuts
and eye infections. The powdered herb can
be taken as snuff.

HERB BENNET

WOOD AVENS, GOLDY STAR, CLOVE-ROOT,
HERB OF ST BENEDICT

Height 30–60cm/12–24in ❀ May–October

Geum urbanum
L *geum* from Gk *geno*, fragrant;
L *urbanum*, related to towns

A perennial plant with a stout woody rhizome.
Leaves at base pinnate, with 2–5 pairs of
unequal leaflets, the terminal one largest.
Stem leaves longer, almost trefoil. All leaves
toothed. Upright small yellow flowers, on
individual stems, with long green sepals
interspacing petals. Fruits in round cluster like
a bur, each seed hooked for animal dispersal.

Roots have a delicate clove-like aroma used
to repel moths and flies, and to flavour ale and
Benedictine liqueur. Infusion taken against
diarrhoea, stomach and liver upsets, and
as a mouthwash. Highly recommended by
Culpeper. Added to bath water, it heals cuts
and piles.

LETTUCE, WALL

Height 30–60cm/12–24in ❀ July–September

Mycelis muralis
L *mycelium*, mushroom spores;
muralis, growing on walls

A hairless slender upright perennial with a
solitary branched purplish stem with milky
juice inside. Soft deeply lobed leaves, upper
ones clasping the stem, have red veins. The
upper lobes are roughly triangular. Similar to
Nipplewort, but that has leaves lobed only at
base. Flowers arranged in a broad, loose bunch
of 5-petalled florets; compare Nipplewort,
which has many rays round a crowded
Dandelion-like head. Fruits like little
parachutes of white hair.

Its use as a salad plant is indicated by its
name. An earlier name for the genus was
Lactuta from the Latin for milk, which referred
to the sap.

41

MEADOW RUE, LESSER

Height 22–60cm/9–24in ✤ July–September

Thalictrum minus
Gk name for the plant; L *minus*, lesser
Rue from the bitterness of its taste

An almost hairless perennial. Slender wiry
stems bear dainty leaves reminiscent of
Maidenhair Fern, leaflets 3 to 4 pinnate,
irregularly lobed. Clusters of tiny drooping
flowers with long greenish-yellow stamens.
Whole plant has a feathery appearance.
Widely distributed in Europe except the
far north.

Gerard suggests that eaten pickled, or with
honey and fennel, it improves eyesight; heated
juice cures earache. He quotes Dioscorides:
'Rue put up the nostrils stems bleeding,' and
Pliny: 'Rue beaten and drunk with wine is an
antidote to poisons, or anointed with its juice
repels serpents.'

MULLEIN, GREAT

AARON'S ROD, BEGGAR'S BLANKET, CUDDYLUGS,
SHEPHERD'S STAFF, HAG'S TAPERS

Height 30–200cm/12–80in ✤ June–August

Verbascum thapsus
From L *barbascum*, bearded; *Thapsus*, place in
Sicily where it grew

A sturdy downy upright biennial with a basal
rosette of large blunt leaves. Stem closely
clasped by narrower downy leaves that overlap
each other. Large yellow flowers have 3 hairy
upper stamens, 2 smooth lower stamens.
Anthers orange. Egg-shaped fruit capsule
contains seeds.

Flowers, without calices, make medicine for
coughs, gripe, piles and consumption in cattle.
Flowers and young leaves in infusion taken for
cramp and gout; good for bathing open wounds.
Other parts of this plant are poisonous. Flowers
yield a yellow hair dye. The Romans called it
Candelaria, from their practice of using the
stems dipped in suet as candles.

ORCHID, LADY'S SLIPPER

Height 20–60cm/8–24in ✽ May–June

Cypripedium calceolus
Gk *cypris*, Venus; *pedilon*, slipper;
L *calceolus*, a small shoe

A striking orchid, the largest in Britain, once
not uncommon in parts of Yorkshire, County
Durham and Westmorland. After germination
it is 4 years before it produces leaves and 16
before it flowers. Mature plants reproduce
from creeping underground rhizomes. Upright
stems bear up to 5 broad leaves, like Lily
of the Valley, headed by one or two large
nodding flowers. Claret-coloured petals and
sepals contrast with a yellow sac-like lip (the
'slipper'), spotted red inside, a trap for insects
seeking nectar. Grows naturally in limestone
woods. Protected newly planted specimens
can be seen on the public Waterfalls Walk
at Ingleton, North Yorkshire.

OXLIP, FALSE

Height 10–30cm/4–12in ✽ April–June

Primula veris × vulgaris
L *primus*, first (to bloom)
Oxlip from AS *oxenslyppe*, ox slop

A perennial hybrid, probably a primrose
impregnated by a cowslip. Toothed wrinkly
leaves, rounded and tapered towards the base.
Hairy stem usually shorter than cowslip with
larger flatter flowers, deeper yellow at centres,
not drooping to one side. Plants usually found
singly, not in masses, where both Cowslip and
Primrose occur.

    Rhizome and roots, but not flowers, used
for bronchitis, coughs, colds and flu. In East
Anglia, the related True Oxlip was believed
to grow only on wild boar dung; as wild boar
declined, so did this plant. Gerard says: 'the
flowers are not so thick thrust together and
they are fairer, and not so many in number,
and do not smell so pleasant [as Primroses
and Cowslips].'

PANSY, MOUNTAIN

Height 7–20cm/3–8in ❀ **April–August**

Viola lutea
L *viola*, name for violets and pansies; *lutea*, yellow
Pansy from Fr *pensée*, thought

A hairless perennial with creeping underground branched rootstocks that throw up flowering stems at intervals. Flower stems short. Leaves bluntly toothed, oval to lance-shaped; upper ones narrower with lobes. Yellow flowers with lower petals deeply veined, and with much shorter sepals. Fruit a capsule that splits into 3 to disperse seeds. In Teesdale, the same species may be deep violet or bicoloured. Grows on lime-rich uplands, usually in sheep pastures. Differs from Heartsease (*V. tricolor*) by having larger flowers, 2.5cm/1in long, with a spur 2 to 3 times as long as the sepal appendages.

Medicinal uses now remote, possibly similar to Heartsease. It has long been used in the breeding of garden pansies.

PEPPER, WALL

BITING STONECROP

Height 5–10cm/2–4in ❀ **June–July**

Sedum acre
L *sedum*, to sit; *acre*, sharp-tasting

A succulent perennial evergreen with fibrous roots that penetrate tiny crevices to form mats even on rocks. Alternate fleshy swollen leaves are broadest at the bottom. Bright yellow starry flowers held in branched clusters, each with 5 pointed petals. Yellow fruits turn brown.

A homeopathic remedy for piles and anal infections. Bruised plant used to be applied to wounds and burns, and is alleged to soften corns and calluses. Pliny said that wrapped in a black cloth and put under the pillow unawares it aided sleep. The leaves taste of pepper and the plant is slightly poisonous – dizziness, headaches, nausea and vomiting are unpleasant side effects. Grown on cottage roofs, it was supposed to protect against lightning and witches.

PRIMROSE

SIMMERINS (YORKSHIRE), EASTER ROSE,
BUTTER ROSE

Height 5–15cm/2–6in   ❀ March– June

Primula vulgaris
L *primus*, first; *vulgaris*, common

A perennial with a low rosette of crinkly oval
leaves tapered to the base, softly downy below.
Pale yellow solitary flowers, slightly darker at
throat. Highly scented. Sticky seeds carried
by ants to germinate where dispersed. Prefers
shady locations such as woods, coppices, under
hedges, usually on heavy soils.

   Primrose tea taken for rheumatism, gout,
arthritis and migraine. Root decoction used
against coughs, catarrhs, bronchitis, headache,
jaundice and ringworm. Flowers used in love
potions, to drive out worms and to dye eggs at
Easter; also to decorate salads and sweets and,
crystallised, in puddings. On May Eve, houses
and barns were decorated with primroses to
protect the occupants, including animals.

RAGWORT

RAGWEED, STINKING WILLIE, ST JAMES WORT,
MARE'S FART

Height 30–120cm/12–48in   ❀ June–October

Senecio jacobaea
L *senex*, old man; *jacobaea*, relating to
St James, patron saint of horses

A hairless biennial with furrowed erect much-
branched stems. Lower leaves stalked and
deeply pinnate; upper leaves clasp stem. Flat
clusters of yellow daisy-like flowers have a
ragged look. Seeds have parachutes of white
hairs.

   Leaves contain an alkaloid poison that
destroys the liver, yet was once used in a mild
infusion to cure 'staggers', an infection of the
brain and spinal cord of domestic animals. A
noxious weed for farmers and stock keepers.
The Irish and Scots believed fairies rode the
stalks; later witches took over! The national
emblem of the Isle of Man. (Illustration, right,
shows browsing larva of the Cinnabar Moth.)

ROCK-ROSE

SUN FLOWER, SUN ROSE

Height 5–30cm/2–12in ☀ May–October

Helianthemum (H. chamaecistus)
Gk *helios*, sun; *anthemum*, flower; *chamae*,
creeping; *cistus*, shrub

A prostrate evergreen sub-shrub. Branches
spread from a woody base. Small lance-shaped
leaves, often curled over and with small
stipules at base, green above, greyish and hairy
below. 5-petalled golden-yellow flowers in
groups of up to 12 per stem, often with an
orange blotch at base of petals. Grows on
rocky or grassy limestone. The unscented
flowers open in sunshine. In dull weather, the
closed petals push pollen-covered stamens on
to the style for self-pollination.

According to Pliny, the wise men of Cilicia
and the Kings of Persia anointed their bodies
with *Helianthemum* boiled with lion's fat, a
little saffron and date wine to make them
'handsome'.

ROCK-ROSE, HOARY

Height 5–30cm/2–12in ☀ May–July

Helianthemum canum
L *canum*, white, hairy

A compact low-lying mat-forming sub-shrub.
Its silvery hairy leaves are narrower than the
Common Rock-Rose, and its erect stem bears
only 3 to 5 flowers of half the size. There are
no stipules or small sub-leaves at the bases
of leaves. As with the Common Rock Rose,
long, sensitive stamens move to rub against
visiting insects to distribute pollen. A relict
of the Late Glacial period, this rare plant is
found in limestone areas of Northern England,
Wales and the Burren in Galway; also in
Sweden, Germany and France.

No recorded medicinal, culinary or other
use.

SAGE, WOOD

HIND HEAL, GIPSY'S BACCY

Height 15–30cm/6–12in ❀ July–November

Teucrium scorodonia
Gk Teucer, a king of Troy, who used it
medicinally; *scorodonia*, garlic

A downy perennial ascending from a slender
rhizome. Erect branched stems are square and
hairy. Heart-shaped leaves in pairs up stems
are toothed and wrinkled as in culinary sage.
Flowers in pairs at top of stems have pale
yellow lower lip with 5 lobes but no upper lip,
leaving brown stamens exposed. The sepal
tube, swollen at the base, carries 4 smooth
seeds.

A common ingredient in tonic wines. It is
a diuretic and wound herb; tea made from it
eases rheumatism. It can, however, cause liver
damage. With a smell and taste like hops, it
gives a bitter flavour to beer and clarifies it
to bestow a rich colour. In Jersey, it is called
Ambroise after the nectar of the gods.

ST JOHN'S WORT, HAIRY

DEVIL'S BANE

Height 30–90cm/12–36in ❀ June–September

Hypericum hirsutum
Gk *hyper*, above; *eikon*, picture (hung to deter
evil spirits); L *hirsutum*, hairy

A hairy perennial with a creeping root. Its
stout round hairy stem may have two raised
ridges. Stalkless, opposite leaves have clear
veins and translucent, puncture-like glands.
Large clusters of dainty yellow 5-petalled
flowers with black dots on the edges of the
pointed green sepals. Fruit is a 3-celled capsule.

The Knights of St John used it to heal
wounds. A cough cure, helpful for catarrh
and bed-wetting; stimulates the kidneys. A
magical herb, used as a charm against fairies,
the devil and lightning. Still used against
depression, although recent warnings suggest
that over-use can be dangerous when taken
with other medications. The family badge of
the McKinnons.

SILVERWEED

GOOSE TANSY, BREAD AND CHEESE

Height 5–25cm/2–10in   ❀ May–August

Potentilla anserina
L *potens*, powerful; *anserina*, relating to geese

A creeping perennial with a branched stock producing rooting stolons in the same way as strawberries. Pinnate leaves have 6–12 pairs of toothed hairy leaflets, alternating large and small. Solitary long-stalked flowers have 5 yellow notched petals twice as long as sepals.

Same medical uses as Creeping Cinquefoil, and used in a number of proprietary medicines. Plant steeped in buttermilk removes freckles. Less astringent than Tormentil and gentler with diarrhoea. Before potatoes were known in Europe, roots were eaten boiled, raw, or dried and ground into meal for bread and porridge. John Ray wrote in 1670 that the children around Settle dug them up and ate them, saying they tasted like parsnip.

SPIKENARD, PLOUGHMAN'S

HORSE HEAL, CINNAMON ROOT

Height 15–120cm/6–48in   ❀ July–October

Inula conyza
L name for Elecampane; Gk *conyza*, dust or powder (for insecticide)
Spikenard, a costly aromatic ointment from the East; Ploughman's, humble

An erect, hairy, perennial, purplish stem branched mainly at top. Leaves like fox-glove, finely toothed, upper ones unstalked. Small numerous flower-heads dull yellow, usually unrayed, with purple inner flower bracts in a flat cluster. Seeds are tiny parachutes.

Similar medicinal qualities to *I. helenium*: used as an infusion for bronchitis, stomach disorders, gall bladder problems, lack of appetite and anorexia. Not in common use. Gerard called it Cinnamon Root because of its aroma. Once hung up to drive away fleas and gnats.

THISTLE, CARLINE

BOAR'S THROAT, EVERLASTINGS

Height 15–30cm/6–12in   July–October

Carlina vulgaris
Named after Charlemagne

A stiff prickly biennial with a branched stem
and a rosette only in its first year. Alternate
stem leaves, prickly, thistle-like, lower ones
downy. Flowers, solitary or up to 5, rayless but
with spiny leaf-like outer bracts like rays that
fold over in rain. The fawn-coloured dead
flowers last all winter.

    When Charlemagne's army suffered from
plague, an angel told him to fire an arrow
for a cure. It landed on this thistle, which he
used to treat and heal his men. Mildly diuretic
and antibiotic, it stimulates perspiration and
relieves spasms. The root stock, collected in
autumn and shredded or semi-dried, is still
used in some brands of proprietary medicine
for gall bladder and digestive disorders.

TORMENTIL

BLOOD ROOT (NORTHUMBERLAND)

Height 5–50cm/2–20in   May–October

Potentilla erecta
L *potens*, powerful (medicinal); *erecta*, upright
(flower stems)

A slender prostrate perennial rising from a
woody root stock. Basal trefoil leaves usually
die before flowering occurs. Stem leaves have
three stalkless leaflets with 2 stipules at base
making them look 5-fingered, toothed near
tip, silver beneath. Numerous 4-petalled
yellow flowers with red centres separated by
4 thin sepals. Up to 2 seeds in a small cup.
An acid-loving plant, but grows happily on
rain-leached soil in limestone areas.

    Strongly astringent, it was named Tormentil
from its wide use to ease the torment of
toothache. Dried rhizome used against
diarrhoea, as a decoction or in a powdered
form against intestinal inflammation, or as
an oral antiseptic in gargles and toothpaste.

TREFOIL, BIRD'S FOOT

BACON AND EGGS, LADY'S SHOES AND
STOCKINGS, CROW-TOES, OVER 70 UK
LOCAL NAMES

Height 10–40cm/4–16in ❀ **May–September**

Lotus corniculatus
Gk plant name; L *corniculatus*, horned

A sprawling perennial with solid stems rising
from a woody rootstock. Shamrock-like leaves
with 2 stipules below. Up to 7 flowers form a
flat circular head above a longish stalk. Pea-
like flowers yellow, often with red streaks,
have a beaked keel. The fruits are in straight
pods that twist as they open to release their
seeds, making the fruit head appear like a
bird's foot. Usually found in short grass or
roadside verges.

One of its local names was No Blame: in
Ireland, children used to carry it to school
in the belief that it would help them avoid
punishment.

ANEMONE, WOOD

WINDFLOWER, THUNDER FLOWER,
SMELL FOXES

Height 5–30cm/2–12in   ❀ March–June

Anemone nemorosa
Gk *Anemone* from Adonis, also known as
Naamen; *nemorosa*, of the woods

Slender stems rise from underground tubers.
Two-thirds up stem is a ring of 3 leaves, each
with 3 toothed segments. White flowers
tinged pink open only in sunshine. Seed head
is a ball of 10–30 downy fruits. Musky smell.
An ancient woodland indicator. Pheasants
eat the flowers.

 Leaves made into vinegar for poultices and
for washing ulcers and sores. Gerard prescribed
bathing with a decoction of leaves for leprosy,
chewing the roots for dispelling lethargy, and
ointment made from the leaves for clearing
ulcers and inflamed eyes. Used rarely now,
except as an external palliative for arthritis.
Juice, especially of roots, bitter and poisonous.

BANEBERRY

HERB CHRISTOPHER, TOADROOT, BUGBANE

Height 30–60cm/12–24in   ❀ May–June

Actaea spicata
Gk *actaea*, elder (leaf shape); L *spicata*, spiked
(flowers)
Baneberry from AS *bana*, murderer (poisonous)

Perennial with a long thick creeping black
root. Large, dusky, toothed, trifoliate dark
green leaves similar to Elder, but has smaller
stem leaves. Strong-smelling. Erect branched
flower stem rising directly from the roots bears
short feathery oblongs of small white flowers
with 4–6 petals. Very poisonous green berries
shaped like rugby balls turn black when ripe.
Rare. Cumbria, Yorkshire and Lancashire only,
in lime-stone grykes.

 Leaves believed to be good for breast
tumours and inflammation, roots for catarrh
and some nervous conditions. Mixed with
alum, the roots produce a black dye.

BEDSTRAW, LIMESTONE

STERNER'S BEDSTRAW

Height 5–10cm/2–4in ☸ June–July

Galium sterneri
Gk *gala*, milk; Sterner, botanist who first
identified it

A low perennial with a mat of shoots and
ascending flower stems. Pointed narrowly
oblong leaves in whorls of 7–8 with backward-
pointing bristles along margins. Creamy-white
flowers in broad pyramidal clusters. Flowers
smaller than Heath Bedstraw. Fruits pairs of
warty seeds (like small Cleavers). As its name
suggests, it thrives on limestone, but may also
be found on volcanic rocks in north-western
Europe. It is believed to be commoner in
Cumbria than anywhere else in Britain.

No trace of herbal usage, but probably used
as an inferior strewing herb.

BURNET SAXIFRAGE

LESSER BURNET, OLD MAN'S PLAYTHING,
BENNET

Height 30–60cm/12–24in ☸ July–September

Pimpinella saxifraga
L *pimpinella*, bipinella, with 2-pinnate leaves;
saxifraga, stone-breaker

A downy branched perennial with a stout
rootstock. Its tough stem is lightly ridged.
Leaves at base like Salad Burnet, broad
coarsely toothed leaflets. Upper leaves finely
cut. 5-petalled white flowers in umbels like
Pignut. Oval fruits.

It is not a Saxifrage (nor a Burnet), but
sixteenth-century apothecaries believed
potions would break gall and kidney stones.
Infusions from dried roots used for coughs,
bronchitis and laryngitis. Used as a gargle for
tonsillitis, ulcers and infected gums. Roots
chewed to relieve toothache and paralysis of
the tongue. Its bitter essential resin is used in
Germany to add blue coloration to brandy.

DAISY

BAIRNWORT, BRUISEWORT

Height 4–10cm/2–4in ❀ March–November

Bellis perennis
L *bellis*, pretty; *perennis*, perennial

An evergreen perennial with a rosette of broad spoon-shaped, slightly toothed shiny ground-hugging leaves. Flowers, borne singly, have a yellow disc of rayless florets surrounded by white-rayed florets, often tipped crimson. Named 'day's eye' because it closes at night.

Infusions of flowers used for catarrh, rheumatics, liver and kidney disorders, diarrhoea and blood conditions. Leaves applied to bruises. Young buds and leaves eaten in salads, buds pickled as capers. Daisy chains are a protection against fairies, hence the Scottish name Bairnwort. The flower is worn on Empire Day, 24 May.

DAISY, DOG

OX-EYE DAISY, HORSE DAISY, MOONFLOWER, MARGUERITE, MOON DAISY

Height 30–60cm/12–24in ❀ June–October

Chrysanthemum leucanthemum
Gk *chrysos*, gold; *anthos*, flower; L *leucanthus*, white-flowered (rays)

A slightly hairy unbranched perennial. A ridged hairy stem rises from a stout tuber. Deeply toothed paddle-shaped leaves have long tapering stalks. Narrower upper leaves clasp stem. Solitary flower heads have yellow disc florets, outer ones with white rays. Sepals green, edged brown. Brown nutlet seeds.

Peachey recommended it as cure for asthma and consumption, wounds and ulcers. Used in salves and medicines for many diseases, including chest and liver complaints. On Colonsay, a remedy for scrofula (King's Evil). Stem juice used as drops for runny eyes.

DROPWORT

Height 15–45cm/6–18in ❀ May–August

Filipendula vulgaris
L *filum*, thread; *pendulus*, hanging (refers to threads connecting root tubers); *vulgaris*, common

Tubers develop on a thread-like root away from parent. Erect stem with dark green toothed pinnate leaves, mainly as a basal rosette. Light cream flowers with 6 petals, purplish below, unscented. Buds globular, like dewdrops. Downy nutlet fruits ribbed but not twisted like Meadowsweet. This is the limestone grassland form of Meadowsweet, with fewer, unscented flowers.

EYEBRIGHT

OCULARIS, OPHTHALMICA

Height up to 30cm/12in ❀ June–September

Euphrasia officinalis
From Euphrosyne, Gk Grace of gladness and mirth; L *officinalis*, from herb store or pharmacy

A hairy annual with erect stems rising from a creeping branch. Toothed oval leaves, dark green and hairy. Flowers 2-lipped in leafy spikes. Lower lip has 3 narrow lobes, and purple lines leading to a yellow patch. Lilac upper lip also lined.

In the sixteenth century, William Coles said its resemblance to a bloodshot eye indicated a cure for eye diseases. Culpepper said drops in the eye improved eyesight and memory, and these are still widely sold by herbalists. Bitter and astringent, it is made into poultices for coughs, colds, sore throats and catarrh. It is also an ingredient in mixed herbal tobaccos used for asthma.

FLAX, FAIRY

PURGING FLAX, LADY'S LINT

Height 5–20cm/2–8in ❀ May–October

Linum catharticum
L *linum*, flax, linen; *catharticum*, purging

An erect slender annual with wiry stems rising
from threadlike roots bearing opposite leaves,
each with a single vein. White, 5-petalled
flowers are borne in a loose branched head.
Fruits, almost spherical, have tiny brown
seeds. Grows on upland pastures mainly in
limestone areas, and is common throughout
the Lakes and Dales.

A purgative, emetic, diuretic and worm
cure. A tincture of the whole plant is used
against bronchitis, piles and amenorrhoea,
and was once taken as an infusion against liver
disorders, constipation and rheumatic pains.
Not now used because its effect is too violent.

GROMWELL

GREY MILLET

Height 20–100cm/8–40in ❀ June–July

Lithospermum officinale
L *litho*, stone; *spermum*, seeds; *officinale*,
apothecary's herb
Gromwell from OFr *gromil*, grey millet

A rough hairy perennial of the Borage family.
Erect ovate stems bear numerous unstalked
pointed lance-shaped rough leaves with
prominent veins. Small creamy-white flowers
are borne terminally and in loose spikes in
the leaf axils. Fruits consist of 4 glossy white
nutlets. Grows mainly in limestone areas,
especially along the South Lakeland coast,
and found rarely on waste ground in the Dales.

The powdered seeds have been used for the
treatment of kidney stones and arthritis, and
to reduce fevers.

JACK BY THE HEDGE

GARLIC MUSTARD, HEDGE GARLIC

Height 30–60cm/12–24 in   ✾ April–July

Alliaria petiola
L *aria*, resembling *allium*, garlic; *petiola*, stalked

An erect unbranched perennial plant with
stalked heart-shaped leaves near base,
triangular above. When crushed they emit
a garlic odour. Erect stem bears a cluster of
small white flowers whose pungent garlic
smell attracts midges and hoverflies. Erect
fruits in long green seed pods. In June this
plant attracts the pale green caterpillars of
the Orange Tip butterfly.

A diuretic, kills worms. Infusion helps
bronchitis, eczema and other skin disorders.
Herbal compress for cuts and skin ailments.
Leaves in salads give a garlic flavour without
making the breath smell, and a mustardy
aftertaste. Makes a good sauce for fish dishes.

LILY OF THE VALLEY

MAY LILIES, OUR LADY'S TRESSES

Height 6–21cm/2.5–8.5in   ✾ May–July

Convallaria majalis
L *convallis*, valley; *majalis*, of May

Perennial with a long creeping rhizome.
Leaves in pairs, lower ones sheathing the
stem. Very fragrant white flowers, small
pendulous bells on a one-sided raceme, the 3
sepals and petals fused into one. Seeds encased
in bright red globular berries which are VERY
POISONOUS. Does not fruit often, multiplies
mainly by its creeping rhizome.

Contains a drug similar to digitalis but non-
poisonous, used in homeopathy and allopathy
for heart conditions and to restore speech after
cardiac arrest. Medieval herbalists used it to
strengthen the brain, renovate the memory,
and for eye inflammation. The flowers have
long been symbols of happiness, purity and
gentleness.

MEADOWSWEET

BRIDEWORT, QUEEN OF THE MEADOW

Height 60–120cm/24–48in ☀ June–September

Filipendula ulmaria
L *filum*, thread (roots); *ulmus*, elm (which the leaves resemble)

Clusters of stems rise from tubers. Dark green leaves, whitish below, are crumpled and wrinkled like Elm leaves. Each leaf has up to 5 pairs of leaflets. Purplish, rising to pale green, stems bear frothy upright clusters of 5-petalled flowers with an almond scent. Fruits are fused together into a spiral (its old name was *Spiraea*). Common in woods and damp places.

A strewing herb, especially for weddings, also used in brides' garlands and posies. Contains salicylic acid, i.e. aspirin. Used against diarrhoea, toothache, rheumatism and influenza. The root was once used for flour, and dried flowers make tobacco.

MOUNTAIN EVERLASTING

CAT'S PAW, CAT'S FOOT

Height 7–20cm/3–8in ☀ June–July

Antennaria dioica
L *antenna*, male flowers have hairs like butterflies' antennae; *dioica*, double house (male and female on separate plants)

A perennial with stems rising at nodes from a creeping woody root. Rosette of grey-green spoon-shaped leaves, silvery below. Erect flowering stems have alternate stem-hugging narrow leaves. White male flower has rays like a daisy; pink female flower is more bunched, erect and rayless. Growing on rock, it gathers soil around it until over-richness kills it. Fossilised remains from over 10,000 years ago found in Rockies.

Used as a diuretic and against diarrhoea; kills worms. Used in proprietary medicines for renal and rheumatic disorders.

NIGHTSHADE, ENCHANTER'S

CINDERELLEN, PHILTREWORT, WITCHES'
POISON

Height 15–70cm/6–27in ❀ June–August

Circaea lutetiana
Gk Circe, beautiful witch who turned Ulysses'
crew into pigs; L *Lutetiana*, Paris

A slightly downy perennial with long slim
stolons. Erect hairy stems have opposite,
toothed, pointed oval leaves with a channel
along top edge. Leafless spikes of sparse flowers
with 2 petals deeply notched and 2 lobed
stigma. Hairy fruits have hooks for clinging
to animals. Belongs to the Willowherb family.
    Always associated with magic, the Angles
called it Aelfthone, a protection against elves.
Being rich in tannin, it may have been used as
an astringent.

ORCHID, GREATER BUTTERFLY

FOXSTONES

Height 20–60cm/8–24in ❀ May–June

Platanthera cholorantha
L *platanthera*, flat antlers; Gk *chloranthus*,
green-flowered

Twin tubers, each forked. A new tuber formed
annually as old one dies away. One pair of
shiny basal leaves and pairs of narrower
unstalked pointed leaves alternate up stem.
Vanilla-scented flowers. White narrow oval
petals, lower one a strap-like lip, and a
2.5cm/1in down-curved spur. Loose spike of
10–15 flowers. Persists a long time, especially
in shade where flowers are greener. Insect
pollinated.
    Gerard classified it under Foxstones,
considering it of no great use in physic.
The night-scented Lesser Butterfly Orchid
(*Platanthera bifolia*) is smaller, with a much
narrower, crowded spike with closely parallel
pollen bunches.

PENNYCRESS, ALPINE

Height 7.5–30cm/3–12 in   April–July

Thlaspi caerulescens or *T. alpestre*
Gk *thlaspi*, name of similar plant;
L *caerulescens*, sky blue

A hairless greyish perennial with a basal
rosette of stalked elliptical leaves with smaller
heart-shaped upper leaves alternately clasping
stem. A loose cluster of white flowers with
prominent purple anthers develop into narrow
heart-shaped winged seed pods. A delicate,
pale purplish-looking plant that, like Spring
Sandwort, has the ability to thrive on soil
polluted with lead mine waste. It accumulates
metals such as lead, zinc and nickel, which
helps to decontaminate the ground.
Commonly found near old lead workings
in the Lakes and Dales, but also occurs
on limestone, whinstone and other rocky
outcrops. Elsewhere occurs in similar habitats
in areas round Alston, the Peak District
and Snowdonia.

PIGNUT

EARTHNUT, STINKY LIPS

Height 22–45cm/9–18in   May–July

Conopodium majus
Gk *conos*, cone (root shape); *podium*, foot

Round brown tuber bears erect, slightly ridged
stem with carrot-like leaves that die back
before flowering stem emerges with fine leaves
rising from a strong sheath. Loose clusters of
notched white flowers similar to, but more
delicate than, Burnet Saxifrage. Beaked oval
fruits. Common in dry pastures. The 'nuts'
grow about 20cm/8in below ground.

Root tuber can be eaten raw, or cooked to
give a parsnip-like flavour. Much loved and
rooted out by pigs which were once trained
like truffle-hunters to locate them for human
consumption. Caliban offered to dig up
pignuts with his long nails for his master
Prospero.

RAMSONS

WILD GARLIC, RAMPS

Height 8–45cm/3–18in ❀ April–July

Allium ursinum
Gk *allium*, garlic; L *ursus*, bear (fit only for bears to eat)

An odorous bulbous woodland perennial. Two or 3 bright green ovate leaves with parallel veins appear first, then an erect, round, three-sided stem bearing a loose ball of white starry flowers with pointed petals and prominent stamens. Fruit is globe-shaped in a 3-lobed ovary. Seeds are black.

Fresh leaves may be eaten raw in salads for high blood pressure. Used as a flavouring in soups and with vegetables. Has similar properties to clove garlic but leaves a bitter aftertaste.

The name Ramsbottom means Ramson Valley; Ramsey means Ramson Island.

SANDWORT, SPRING

LEADWORT

Height 5–15cm/2–6in ❀ May–September

Minuartia verna
After Juan Minuart (1693–1768), botanist from Barcelona; L *verna*, spring

A dainty low cushion-forming perennial, often hairy with 3-veined pointed and keeled leaves in tufts up slender stems. Loose clusters of 2–7 white flowers, 5-petalled with purple anthers, petals longer than white-edged sepals. Grows up to great altitudes, in dry stony places in lime-rich soils. In the Yorkshire Dales it is known as Leadwort, because it is an early coloniser of land polluted by mineral spoil principally from lead mines.

No known medical uses.

SANICLE

Height 20–60cm/8–24in ❀ May–August

Sanicula europaea
L *sanicula*, little healer, a corruption of
St Nicholas, a great healer

Hairless perennial with long-stemmed, shiny,
deeply-cut 5 lobed toothed leaves. Short
staked clusters of pinkish-white flowers.
Roundish fruits covered in clinging hooked
bristles.

    Called Herbe de St Laurent in France,
it is invoked for burns and scalds because
St Laurence was put to death on a grid-iron.
A vulnerary, it was applied to wounds and
bleeding, both internal and external, and
used for skin diseases, mouthwashes, chest
complaints, coughs, catarrh and piles. A
fifteenth-century apothecaries' cure-all drink
was made of Sanicle, Yarrow and Bugle: 'Bugle
holdeth it open, Mylfoyle clensith, Sanicle
helith.'

SAXIFRAGE, RUE-LEAVED

THREE-FINGERED SAXIFRAGE

Height 3–8cm/1–3in ❀ April–May

Saxifraga tridactylites
L *saxum*, rock; *frango*, to break (rock or
gallstones?); *tridactyl*, three-fingered

A small, sticky, hairy annual. Erect stems bear
often reddish 3- to 5-fingered leaves on short
stalks, divided for flowers. Small 5-petalled
white flowers on own stalks. Seeds are egg-
shaped. Grows on walls, rocks or dry limy
places up to at least 550m/1,800ft, the top of
the Main Limestone of the Yorkshire Dales.

    No known medicinal or culinary uses.

SNOWDROP

SNOW PIERCER, FEBRUARY FAIRMAIDS,
CANDLEMAS BELLS, DINGLE DANGLE

Height 15–25cm/6–10in ❀ February–March

Galanthus nivalis
Gk *gala*, milk; *anthos*, flower; L *nivalis*, of snow

Perennial bulb bearing long linear grooved
and keeled grey-green hairless leaves. Round
stems carry single nodding white flowers with
a greenish hood. Three larger outer petals
white, 3 bell-like notched inner petals green
outside, white with green tip inside. Green
anthers. Seeds in a green egg-shaped capsule.
Grows in woodlands and by stream sides. A
native of Southern Europe, introduced from
Italy.
  Once used for digestive disorders. In the
Victorian language of flowers, the snowdrop
is a symbol of purity. It is associated with
Candlemas on 2 February, the feast of the
Purification of the Virgin Mary, when it is
in flower.

SOLOMON'S SEAL, ANGULAR

VAGABOND'S FRIEND

Height 15–25cm/6–10 in ❀ May–July

Polygonatum odoratum
Gk *poly*, many; *gony*, knees; L *odoratum*,
scented

Angled arching stems rise from a thick jointed
rhizome. Alternate pointed oval leaves
without stalks rise in opposite rows. Scented
single or paired white flowers grow from
the leaf angles, hanging to one side but not
waisted as in common Solomon's Seal. Fruit
a poisonous black berry. South Lakeland is its
most northerly recorded location in Britain.
  Herbalists used rhizome as a diuretic
and tonic, with stronger infusions for cuts,
bruises, broken bones, eczema and other skin
disorders. Its Lakeland name, Vagabond's
Friend, reflects its effectiveness against black
eyes, broken noses and bruises.

SORREL, WOOD

SPRING BEAUTY, ALLELUJA,
BREAD AND CHEESE

Height 5–15cm/2–6in ❀ March–May

Oxalis acetosalla
Gk *oxys*, acid; L *acetosalla*, acid leaves
Sorrel meaning sour

A perennial with a creeping rhizome. Trefoil
leaves are pale green, purplish below. Solitary
cup-shaped white flowers veined purple with
5 petals. Slender dark stems. Fruit a globular
capsule.

As a medicine it was prescribed for fevers,
scurvy and as an aid in menstruation; bruised
leaves applied to cuts and bruises. Because of
its high oxalic acid content it must be used
sparingly. For centuries it has been used to
add flavour to salads and sauces.

The name Alleluja comes from its
appearance at Easter, and because its three-
in-one leaves signify the Trinity.

STRAWBERRY, BARREN

STRAWBERRY CINQUEFOIL

Height 5–30cm/2–12in ❀ March–June

Potentilla sterilis
L *potens*, powerful (medicinal);
sterilis, sterile, barren

Hairy perennial rising from woody runners.
Blue-green toothed trefoil leaves, grey below.
White flowers, smaller than Wild Strawberry,
have gaps between 4–5 notched petals
revealing pointed green sepals. Seeds in a dry
cluster, lacking the fleshy fruit of the edible
Wild Strawberry. Grows on dry grassland,
hedge bottoms and open woodland.

The root, administered as a powder, is
very astringent; according to Culpepper it is
'excellent in the overflowing of the menses
and in bloody stools'. An infusion of the
young leaves is a diuretic, and it is good for
fevers.

STRAWBERRY, WILD

ALPINE STRAWBERRY

Height 10–20cm/4–8in ❀ May–July

Fragaria vesca
L *fraga*, scent (of fruit); *vesca*, little

A hairy perennial with rooting runners throwing up clumps of toothed trefoil leaves, bright green above, paler below. Flowers on erect stalks have sepals and petals in whorls of 5, with no gaps between petals. Fruit fleshy.

Diuretic, astringent, laxative in small doses. Infusion of leaves taken against arthritis, gall stones, liver and stomach upsets. A tea substitute when spiced with lemon, cinnamon or vanilla and sweetened with honey. (The poisonous leaves of cultivated strawberries must not be used). Feed Blackberry and Strawberry leaves to rabbits and guinea pigs that are off-colour or constipated. The fruit is delectable.

SWEET CICELY

SHEPHERD'S NEEDLE

Height 60–150cm/24–60in ❀ May–June

Myrrhis odorata
Gk plant name; L *odorata*, scented
Cicely from its Gk name *sesel* or after
St Cecilia

A thick carrot-like perennial root supports hollow grooved stems. Large, soft, fern-like leaves smell of aniseed when crushed. Flower head with many stemmed branches has frothy multiple bunches of deeply toothed white flowers. Fruits erect, 2cm/¾in long, ridged, brown.

All parts are edible, with an aniseed flavour. Roots are eaten raw in salads, boiled as vegetable; leaves raw in salads or boiled like spinach. Added to tarts and puddings it acts as a sweetener, especially of tart fruits. In Cumbria the seeds, finely ground and mixed with beeswax, are used as a wood polish.

TRAVELLER'S JOY

OLD MAN'S BEARD, BACCY PLANT, WOODBINE

Stems up to 30m/100ft   ❀ July–September

Clematis vitalba
Gk *clematis*, climbing plant; L *vitalba*, white
vine

A deciduous woody climber with opposite
toothed 3- to 5- leaflet leaves on flexible
stalks which twist around adjacent plants for
suppport. Fragrant greenish-white flowers
have prominent yellow stamens borne in loose
trusses along and at ends of stems. Seeds with
long silvery plumes cluster at stalk heads to
form 'beards'. They persist well into winter.
Grows at woodland edges and in hedgerows
mainly on calcareous ground; fairly common
in South Lakeland.
    Bruised roots and stems boiled in water and
steeped in sweet oil used as a cure for itch.
The stems were once used by boys as a form
of tobacco.

WHITLOW GRASS

SPRING WHITLOW GRASS

Height 3–8cm/1–3in   ❀ March–June

Erophila verna
L *eros*, partly toothed; *phylla*, leaves
Whitlow, OE for white flaw (as in nail
tumours)

Hairy annual, sometimes over-wintering. Basal
rosette of toothed narrow lance-shaped leaves.
Unbranched stem has no leaves. Alternate
flowers on top of stem have deeply notched
white petals. Fruits like miniature Honesty,
each on a long stalk. Farmers in Hereford
took its flowering as a sign to sow their spring
barley. Widespread across Europe.
    Medieval herbalists used it to cure
whitlows. Culpeper advised an infusion of the
fresh plant to 'sweeten the blood and juices,
and scorbutic [scurvy-related] complaints in
general'.

WHITLOW GRASS, HOARY

TWISTED WHITLOW GRASS

Height 8–30cm/3–12in ❀ May–July

Draba incana
Gk *draba*, from a related plant; L *incana*, hoary
or white

A rigid hairy biennial with a rosette of hairy
toothed leaves and smaller toothed leaves
hugging stem all way up. Loose group of
notched white 4-petalled flowers at top.
Oblong elliptical seed pods twist to eject seeds
when ripe. An upland plant, usually growing
above 100m/400ft in European and Asian
limestone screes and cliffs, dunes and
grassland.
  Apart from the use implied by its name, no
medicinal or culinary use has been discovered.

WOODRUFF

STARGRASS, WOODROWELL, WOODROVE

Height 10–45cm/4–18in ❀ April–June

Galium odoratum
Gk *gala*, milk; L *odoratum*, scent
Woodrove from Fr *rovelle*, spur (from shape
of leaves, like the rowel of a spur)

Perennial with a slender creeping rhizome.
Erect 4-sided unbranched stems. Leaves with
prickly margins arranged in whorls of 6–9 up
stem. Pure white flowers in loose heads. Fruits
are hooked with tiny bristles.
  A long-used herb against jaundice, liver
ailments, migraine, bladder complaints,
nerves, insomnia and thromboses. Its scent,
like new-mown hay, increases with time.
Hung in bunches to freshen air, put in drawers
and cupboards to deter moths; used to stuff
pillows. Adds flavour to drinks – in Germany
it is combined with strawberries in hock for a
cooling drink.

CUCKOO PINT

LORDS AND LADIES, WAKE ROBIN,
ADAM AND EVE, SWEETHEARTS

Height 30–45cm/12–18in   ❀ April–May

Arum maculatum
Arum, Gk name; L *maculatum*, spotted
(the spathe)

A fleshy perennial tuber gives rise to stalked
arrow-shaped leaves, often spotted purple or
brown. An upright stem bears a purplish-green
cylindrical flower head surrounded by a spathe
or hood. Pollinated by insects crawling
through down-pointing hairs. Fruits initially
green, turn into orange-red fleshy berries that
are VERY POISONOUS.

Starchy roots can be made into Portland
sago or arrowroot for gruel, and be used as
starch for hair and beards, and for stiffening
clothes (mixing it by hand caused blisters).
Tubers also used as soap; mixed with rose
water, they whiten the skin. The English
names have sexual connotations.

HELLEBORE, STINKING

SETTERWORT, BEARSFOOT

Height 60–80cm/24–32in   ❀ February–April

Helleborus foetidus
Helleborus, Gk name; L *foetidus*, stinking

A stout smelly perennial with evergreen lower
leaves, long-stalked and palmate with toothed
lance-shaped leaflets. Nodding green bell-
shaped flowers have purple rims (inset), and
hang to one side in loose clusters. Fruit is a
cup-shaped capsule containing brown seeds.
Grows on limestone soil.

A dangerously violent purgative once used
against worms in children and as an infusion
for delousing and treating boils, all of which
treatments were frequently fatal. A tincture
has been found useful in nervous disorders and
hysteria. In the Victorian language of flowers
it represented calumny or malicious slander.

HERB PARIS

TRUE LOVE, ONE BERRY, TRUE LOVER'S KNOT

Height 15–40cm/6–16in ❀ May–June

Paris quadrifolia
L *par*, pair (all elements in pairs); *quadrifolia*,
four-leaved

An upright perennial with a creeping rhizome
sprouting single unbranched stems, leafless
except at the top, with 4 pointed-oval leaves
in the shape of a cross. Flowers borne upright
on a 2cm/1in extension, with 4 narrow
yellowish petals, 4 broader green sepals, and 8
erect green stamens with yellow anthers. Fruit
is a red berry-like capsule that turns black
before splitting vertically to disperse red,
shiny, fleshy seeds. An ancient limestone
woodland indicator.
    VERY POISONOUS. Once used in France
as an antidote to some poisons, with fatal
results. The Italian botanist Mattioli
(1501–77) avowed that an unequal numbers
of berries countered witchcraft.

LADY'S MANTLE

LION'S FOOT, NINE HOOKS

Height 5–45cm/2–18in ❀ May–September

Alchemilla vulgaris
From Arab *alkemelych*, plant of the alchemists
who extracted the juice; L *vulgaris*, common

A perennial with a thick woody root-stock,
some leaves sprawling, some upright. Long-
stalked leaves like Sycamore, 7 to 11 lobes and
deeply toothed. Flowers, tiny, yellowish green,
in large leafy clusters (2 rings of 4 sepals).
Many hybrids and variations.
    Dedicated to the Virgin Mary and
traditionally used for women's complaints
including sagging bosoms. Leaves like ladies'
capes gather pearls of dew, suggesting magical
properties. Strong infusions used to treat
diarrhoea. Used as a mouthwash, and for
bathing open sores or wounds. Very astringent.

MERCURY, DOG'S

BOGGART FLOWER (YORKSHIRE), SNAKEWEED

Height up to 40cm/16in ❀ February–May

Mercurialis perennis
Named after Mercury, its alleged discoverer

A creeping perennial with upright
unbranched 4-sided stems, with pairs of
toothed hairy leaves. Insignificant petalless
greenish flowers are female. Male flowers have
identical sepals and petals in whorls of 3. Male
and female on separate plants. Hairy seed has
3 rounded segments.

Once used as a purgative and diuretic.
An essence of the fresh herb was used for
rheumatism, dropsy, diarrhoea, gall and liver
disorders. Culpepper advised the use of it in a
concoction with water and cock chicken for
ague. The leaves must never be eaten. Called
'Dog's' because herbalists considered it unfit
for human use. Once also called Bad Henry, as
opposed to the edible and virtuous Good King
Henry (*Chenopodium bonus-henricus*, Vol. 2).

PELLITORY OF THE WALL

Height 15–38cm/6–15in ❀ June–October

Parietaria judaica
L *paries*, wall; *judaica*, of Judah

A spreading hairy perennial that thrives in
cliff crevices and walls. Stalked red-brown
hairy round stems bear stalked alternate lance-
shaped leaves. Clusters of green female flowers
and yellow male stamens rise from leaf bases.
Seeds are rough clinging nutlets.

Herbalists called it Parritory, and Culpeper
was fulsome about its uses: for coughs,
wheezing, shortness of breath, falling hair,
piles, gout, dropsy, bruises and skin problems,
expelling gall stones, easing maternity pains,
cleansing the skin and dispelling noises in the
ears. It is still used by herbalists as a diuretic
and kidney restorative.

TWAYBLADE

SWEETHEARTS, SWAYBLADE

Height 30–60cm/12–24in ✸ May–July

Listera ovata
Named after Dr M. Lister (1638–1712), palaeontologist; L *ovata*, ovate

An orchid with a short thick creeping rhizome with a large tuft of sinuous roots. Each year the rhizome grows up to a flowering stem, and outward growth continues underground from a lateral bud. A single pair of opposite unstalked oval leaves appear. Long stem bears flower-spike of brown-tinged green flowers. Pollinated by small insects. Germinating seeds need 4 years of mycorhizal support before they can feed themselves, then 10 more years before flowering. Greater dependency on vegetative multiplication. Often flowers in groups.

Discovered by Turner in 1548; he called it Martagon, a Turkish name for a hat. Gerard called it Twayblade and Herb Bifoile, and used it in ointment and balsam for healing wounds.

FELWORT

AUTUMN GENTIAN

Height 5–24cm/2–9in ✤ July–September

Gentianella amarella
After Gentius, 2nd-century King of Illyria
said to have discovered its medicinal uses;
L *amarus*, bitter

An upright perennial with simple or branched
stem. Oval leaves in rosette, stem leaves
opposite and pointed. Dull purple trumpet-
shaped flowers in spikes. Petal tube twice as
long as sepal tube, stays on after flowering.
Fruits cylindrical.

 Used in cures for cramps, King's Evil
(scrofula), bites of mad dogs and venomous
beasts, and loss of appetite. Apothecaries
found this plant just as effective as the Yellow
Gentian, which had been imported in large
amounts from European alpine countries.

ORCHID, EARLY PURPLE

LONG PURPLES, DEAD MEN'S FINGERS,
BLUE BUTCHERS, FOOLSTONES

Height up to 30cm/12in ✤ April–June

Orchis mascula
Gk *orchis*, testicle; *mascula*, male

Twin root tubers, one new and firm for next
year's growth, the other slack supplying
current year's food. Long leaves, often
blotched, at base. Stem carries a loose spike
of purple-crimson flowers, sometimes with a
white throat. 1 sepal and 2 petals form hood,
2 sepals erect and backing towards each other.
Broad lip widens below with small central
lobe. Spur long, curving upwards. Leaf-like
bracts at flower bases.

 Powderised root used against diarrhoea
and as an aphrodisiac. Used in cooking as
arrowroot. Made into salop, a popular drink in
Tudor times – salop houses preceded coffee
houses.

SAXIFRAGE, PURPLE

INGLEBOROUGH BEAUTY, SNOW PURPLE,
MOUNTAIN EMPEROR

Height 5–10cm/2–4in ❀ March–April

Saxifraga oppositofolia
L *saxum*, rock; *frango*, to break; *oppositofolia*,
with opposite leaves

A prostrate perennial with long trailing stems.
Small opposite grey-green leaves, oval, lime-
crusted. Large solitary purplish flowers on very
short stalks, anthers bluish. An arctic alpine
plant at its southern extremity, one of our
earliest flowering plants. Needs damp lime-
rich soils, usually on cliffs. Pollen found in
Teesdale from prehistoric times, but no known
plants remain there now. Widespread in
mountainous Europe but limited in UK
to Cumbria, North Wales, Scotland and
Northern Ireland. A relict species of the
ice age.

SELF HEAL

CARPENTERS' HERB, HOOK HEAL,
SICKLY WORT

Height 5–30cm/2–12in ❀ June–September

Prunella vulgaris
From L *prunum*, purple, or from a cure for
Ger braune (quinsy)

Low patch-forming hairy perennial. Creeping
stem has erect stems with slightly toothed oval
pointed leaves. Purple 2-lipped flowers resting
on spreading pointed bracts are set in regular
tiers in a tight whorl at the top of the stem
above a pair of stalkless leaves. Fruit consists
of 4 small nutlets from each flower.

As the upper lip of the flower is in the
shape of a hook, it was invoked to cure
wounds (made by sickles or bill-hooks).
Used by the Greeks to cure sore throats and
tonsillitis. Can help to lower blood pressure
and is an effective antibiotic against the
sources of urinary infections and enteritis.
An ingredient for spring salads.

THISTLE, MELANCHOLY

SHAVING BRUSH, FISH BELLY

Height 45–120cm/18–48in   ❀ July–September

Cirsium heterophyllum
Gk *cirsium*, thistle; *heterophyllum, different
leaves*

A perennial. Upright grooved stem bears
opposite, toothed lance-shaped leaves, felted
below. Apart from soft spines at leaf edges,
it has no prickles. Large solitary flower heads
droop as buds, hence its name Melancholy,
but become erect as mature red-purple thistle-
type heads. Fruits have parachutes of long
whitish hairs to aid dispersal.

Discovered on Ingleborough by Thomas
Penny in 1581. The Greek physician
Dioscorides said the 'signature' of the
drooping buds offered a charm against sadness.
Culpepper said potion of leaves in wine would
'expel superfluous Melancholy out of the body
and make a man as merry as a cricket'.

THYME, WILD

Height 5–10cm/2–4in   ❀ June–August

Thymus polytrichus
Gk *thumon*, to fumigate (sacrificial);
L *polytrichus*, hairy

A creeping mat-forming perennial with woody
runners. Short square stems have hairs on 2
opposite sides. Short-stalked opposite leathery
leaves, oval with long bristles; round edges
and oil glands on upper surfaces. Undersides
veined. Flowers red-purple in round terminal
heads. A great attraction to honey-seeking
bees and insects.

Highly perfumed and long-lasting, it was
used as a strewing herb. Antiseptic, it is taken
for throat and digestive illnesses, laryngitis
and whooping cough. An infusion rubbed
into the scalp retains hair colour. Its extract,
glycerine of thymol, is used in patent
medicines. Also used in cooking with lamb,
and in bouquet garni, herb butter and herb
vinegar. The family badge of the Drummonds.

AVENS, WATER

GYPSIES' BONNETS, SOLDIERS' BUTTONS

Height 24–40cm/9–16in ❀ April–June

Geum rivale
L *geum*, plant family name; *rivale*, brookside
or water

A downy perennial that rises from a scaly
base. Lower leaves have 3–6 rounded, deeply
lobed leaflets, stem leaves unstalked and
roughly trifoliate on a scarcely branching
stem. Nodding flowers in loose clusters have
pink-cream petals in a purplish-brown cup.
Hooked fruits last a long time. A plant of
northern Britain and northern Europe,
found usually in damp woods, ditches and
hedgerows.
     Herbal properties are similar to Herb
Bennet (*Geum urbanum*; page 41) but less
effective, so it was abandoned as a herbal
medicine. An infusion in water was drunk
as a stomach tonic.

BASIL, WILD

Height 22–45cm/9–18in ❀ July–October

Clinopodium vulgare
Gk *clino*, to slope; L *podion*, foot
Basil from Gk *basilicum*, royal, king of herbs

A hairy aromatic perennial. Erect stems
usually unbranched; oval opposite hairy
leaves, slightly toothed. Faintly scented.
Flowers borne in whorls above leaves with
bristles like bracts that make it look woolly.
Seeds 4 nutlets in a short sepal tube. Grows
on dry grassy banks and in hedgerows on limy
soils.
     Infusion taken for stomach trouble and
enteritis. Indian brahmins eat a few leaves
after meals to aid digestion. Has been used to
preserve cooked meats, and in Egypt it was
scattered over graves. Always popular with
Greek, Italian and French cooks for its hot,
clove-like flavour; used in salads and cooking.

BETONY

BISHOP'S WORT, WOOD BETONY

Height 15–60cm/6–24in   ✤ July–October

Betonica officinalis
From Fr *betoine*, a Gaulish tribe

Perennial herb with a short woody root. Erect hairy stems rise from a persistent basal rosette of stalked toothed ovate leaves. Upper leaves unstalked below 1, often 2, dense cylindrical whorls of reddish-purple labiate (tubular 2-lipped) flowers. Fruits 4, smooth brown tricorn nutlets.

An ancient herbal remedy. Treatise written on it by Emperor Augustus's head physician, Musa, who claimed it would cure 47 diseases. Infusions for diarrhoea, flatulence, flebitis, arthritis, open wounds, headaches and tension, coughs and colds. Dried leaves used as tea, mixed with tobacco and smoked, and as an ingredient for snuff. Once believed to stave off evil spirits.

BISTORT

EASTER LEDGES, PASSION DOCK, ADDERWORT

Height 20–45cm/8–18in   ✤ April–August

Polygonum bistorta
Gk *poly*, many; *gonu*, joints; L *bis*, twice;
torta, twisted (roots)

Perennial plant with a stout contorted rhizome. Erect unbranched stems bear long-stalked basal leaves, upper ones lance-shaped, clutching stem. Single spike of clustered pink flowers in pairs. Fruits like a 3-sided rugby ball. Spreading roots can be invasive.

Roots coiled like a snake suggested a cure for snake-bite. *The Great Herbal* of 1526 recommended Bistort for conception and delivery. A strong astringent and blood purifier. In Northern England, particularly Cumbria, it was boiled with other herbs and served as Easter Ledge Pudding to purge the intestines after a winter-long diet of salted meat and oatmeal.

CENTAURY

BANWORT, BLOODWORT

Height 5–30cm/2–12in   ❀ July–October

Centaurium erythraea
From Gk centaur; *erythro*, red

A hairless annual with a basal rosette of
pointed oval leaves and a few opposite pairs
up stem slightly smaller and veined. Unstalked
pink flowers in terminal clusters on short
branches. Gentian-like flower has 5 narrow
keeled teeth. Fruit capsule longer than calyx.
Common in England, scarcer elsewhere.

Used for arthritis, anaemia, gall and liver
ailments, indigestion, anorexia, hiatus hernia
and fevers. Culpeper said it removed freckles.
A lotion applied to the skin was supposed to
deter fleas and lice. Chaucer in *The Nun's
Priest's Tale* said it was a laxative. The centaur
Chiron was healed by this plant from a wound
inflicted by the 9-headed Hydra.

CRANESBILL, CUT-LEAVED

Height 10–30cm/4–12in   ❀ May–October

Geranium dissectum
Gk *geranos*, crane (bill-like fruit);
L *dissectum*, deeply divided (leaves)

A coarse, often reddish downy annual. Hairy
upright or sprawling stems bear finger-like
leaves jaggedly cut almost to base. Short-
stalked flowers have notched purplish-pink
petals and very hairy sepals with a bristle on
the tips. Downy fruits hold 4 pitted seeds.
These details differentiate it from the rarer
Long-Stalked Cranesbill (*G. colombinum*).
Occurs mainly on disturbed or waste land,
road verges and quarries in South Lakeland,
occasionally in the Yorkshire Dales.

Medicinal uses are as styptic, astringent and
tonic. Taken internally for diarrhoea, cholera
and chronic dysentery. A useful gargle.
Possibly used by early herbalists as a cure
for ruptures.

CRANESBILL, DOVE'S FOOT

MOTHER OF MILLIONS

Height 8–20cm/3–8in ❀ April–September

Geranium molle
Gk *geranos*, crane; L *molle*, soft

Prostrate hairy annual with rounded lobed leaves. Lower leaves have long stalks, upper short-stalked. 5 notched lilac to purple petals and 5 hairy pointed sepals. Seeds in wrinkled case that opens when ripe to eject a seed from each style. Leaf is supposed to resemble a dove's foot, the seed pod a crane's beak.

Culpeper used it for colic, gallstones, inward bleeding, gout or joint ache. As a miraculous cure for ruptures and burstings, Gerard recommended the powdered plant in red wine, with the proviso, 'in aged persons it shall be needful to adde thereto the powder of red snails (those without shells), dried in an oven in number nine . . . that never faileth.'

CRANESBILL, SHINING

ROBIN, BACHELOR'S BUTTONS,
SHINY CRANESBILL

Height 10–30cm/4–12in ❀ May–August

Geranium lucidum
Gk *geranos*, crane; L *lucidum*, shining

A short hairless annual with an erect stem and rounded 5-lobed glossy leaves, often turning red. Pink flowers smaller than Herb Robert in pairs on short stems, with 5 unnotched oval petals and 5 sepals, inflated at the base and ending in a bristle. Hairless fruits in the typical crane's bill shape that splits from the calyx to release the seeds. A common plant of mortared walls, limestone outcrops and roadside verges. A lowland plant found everywhere except in the coastal region; prefers moist shady places.

Any pharmaceutical use is obscure, Herb Robert probably being preferred.

HERB ROBERT

STINKING BOB, DEATH COME QUICKLY

Height 10–50cm/4–20in ❀ **April–December**

Geranium robertianum
Gk *geranos*, crane; species name a corruption
of L *ruber*, red, or after St Robert of Salzburg
or Ruprecht, our Robin Goodfellow

Strong-smelling hairy annual, often reddish,
especially on stems. Triangular fern-like leaves
in 3–5 segments. Pink flowers have 5 rounded
unnotched petals. Fruit slightly wrinkled,
shaped like a crane's beak. Seeds attached
until ripe to a slim filament are smooth;
finches love them. Its strong putrid smell
is attractive to insect pollinators.

By the doctrine of signatures, redness
implied a cure for blood disorders or a means
of stemming blood flow. Used for diarrhoea,
dropsy, gum inflammation and mouth
bleeding. Associated with snakes and
headaches.

MILKMAID

LADY'S SMOCK, CUCKOO FLOWER

Height 15–60cm/6–24in ❀ **April–July**

Cardamine pratensis
Gk *cardamine*, plant name; L *pratensis*,
of meadows

A hairless perennial of damp places. A rosette
of basal leaves, pinnate with a larger terminal
leaflet, upper leaves narrower. Flowers in a
loose bunch held high; 4 notched petals, lilac
to white with deep lilac veins. Anthers yellow.
Seed pods erect like small cucumbers. Often
forms broad colonies in damp spots.

Infusions used against scurvy, dropsy,
epileptic fits and skin ailments. Picking it in
Austria would invite adder bites, in Germany
lightning, in England bad luck, especially if
brought into the house. The young leaves,
shoots and buds taste like watercress and
can be used in salads.

ORCHID, BURNT-TIP

BURNT ORCHID, DWARF ORCHID

Height 10–12cm/4–6in   ✤ May–June

Orchis ustulata
Gk *orchis*, testicle; *ustulata*, burnt

A tiny orchid favouring lime-rich soils. Unlike
most other orchids its seeds exist underground
without roots, wholly dependent on fungus.
A a fleshy mycorhizome swells up in annual
sections to give it a caterpillar look. Ten years
on, it develops tiny roots and the growing tip
bears upwards with 3 pointed-oblong leaves. It
flowers after 13 or more years, when the long
mycorhizome is replaced by a new tuber that
duplicates each following year. The flower
stem bears a few sheathing leaves. An oval
spike is formed by fragrant, browny-purple
hooded, spotted, white-lipped flowers like
typical ginger-bread men. The brownish
unopened buds give it its common name.

Tubers used to make salop for diarrhoea and
biliousness, and to complement limited diets.

ORCHID, EARLY MARSH

SALOP, CUCKOOS

Height 12–24cm/6–12in   ✤ May–July

Dactylhoriza incarnata
Gk *dactylos*, finger; *rhiza*, root; L *incarnata*,
pink or flesh-coloured

The most widespread of the marsh orchids.
Tubers divided into tapering parts and long
spreading roots. Develops quickly, seed to first
leaf in year 2, tuber in year 4, but takes a few
more years to produce 3–10 narrow hooded
leaves and then to flower. Thick, soft, hollow
stem bears a cylindrical spike of small, waxy
pink flowers with two-lobed lips marked with
two loops of darker lines, the sides turned
back, and stout, conical spurs. Bee-pollinated.
Seeds abundantly. Profuse patches on North
Walney.

Used to make the drink salop, especially
useful for undernourished children and for
sailors undertaking long voyages.

ORCHID, FRAGRANT

SCENTED OR CLOVE ORCHID

Height 15–45cm/6–18in ❀ July–August

Gymnadenia conopsea
Gk *gymnos*, naked; *conopsea*, cone-shaped
(tubers)

Double parsnip-like tubers are infected by
mycorhiza to aid nourishment. Aerial stem
rising 3 years after germination has 3–5 long
narrow erect leaves on lower stem, a few
smaller ones further up. Dense flower head
of pink flowers. 3-lobed lip has a long slender
spur. Upper sepals and petals form a hood.
Strong vanilla scent attracts pollinating
insects, with 50–90% successful pollination.
Grows in short turf or on limestone slopes
but is also found on damp peaty ground.
  Any pharmaceutical uses obscure.

ORCHID, PYRAMIDAL

Height 20–45cm/8–18in ❀ July–August

Anacamptis pyramidalis
Anacamptis, plant name; *pyramidalis*, pyramidal

2 round tubers develop from seed over 4 years
aided by fungus. Leaves appear after 5 years,
flowers several years later. Longish fleshy
lower leaves, narrow lance-shaped upper, hug
stem alternately. Unspotted. Pyramid of pink
flowers at first, later cylindrical. Short upper
petals and sepals form hood, deep 3-lobed lip
slopes forward and down. Long slender spur,
same length as ovary. Delicate, musky scent.
Reproduces from seed, 65–95% successful.
Similar in appearance to Fragrant Orchid,
but distinguished by 2 upright ridges on the
lip either side of the mouth of the spur, and
its pair of pollinia being removed together,
not singly.
  No record of pharmaceutical use, but
probably used as an aphrodisiac and aid
to conception.

ORCHID, SPOTTED

PRIEST, SNAKE'S FLOWER, SATYRION,
FINGER ORCHIS

Height 15–60cm/6–24in ☀ July–August

Dactylhoriza fuchsii
Gk *dactylos*, finger; L *rhiza*, root; *fuchsii* after
German botanist Leonhart Fuchs (1501–66)

Old tuber has 4 tapering fingers, new tuber
sac-like. Lowest leaves broad oval, upper
leaves narrower and pointed, up to 8, spotted.
Flower spike up to 13cm/5in long, flowers
variable in colour, mainly pinks. Upper sepals
and petals form a hood, lateral sepals spread
like wings. Broad lip has 3 triangular lobes,
marked with looped lines or spots. Sometimes
found in albino form, white without markings
on petals. Pollinated by bees and flies. Found
in all kinds of soil.

Gerard refers to a Latin name of *Palma
Christi*, after the shape of its tubers.

PRIMROSE, BIRD'S EYE

MEALY PRIMROSE, BONNY BIRD'S EYE

Height 5–15cm/2–6in ☀ May–June

Primula farinosa
L *primus*, first; *farinosa*, mealy

A ground-hugging perennial with a basal
rosette of pale green narrow lance-shaped
leaves with blunt teeth and white below.
Leafless stalk bears a posy of pink, yellow-eyed
5-petalled flowers. Erect cylindrical seeds.
Pollination by insects only. Many of the
flowers and fruits are eaten by sheep. Grows
up to nearly 365m/1,200ft in Teesdale, Craven
and Cumbria. Gerard referred to it as growing
in Westmorland and Lancashire. A smaller
variety known as Scottish Primrose, darker
purple with a yellow eye, grows on the north
coast of Scotland and the Orkneys.

No known pharmaceutical uses.

SQUINANCYWORT

QUINSYWORT

Height 5–10cm/2–4in ☀ June–September

Asperula cynanchica
L *asper*, rough (hairy stems); Gk *kunanchi*,
dog strangler

A prostrate hairless slender perennial. 4 ridges
on stems make them look square. Narrow
lance-shaped leaves in whorls of 4, 2 of them
smaller than the others, up stem. Flowers in
terminal clusters, pink inside, whitish outside,
with long tubed base. Vanilla scented.
Tiny fruits warted. It favours dry pastures on
limestone or chalk, and is at its northern limit
in Cumbria. Found first in 1570 by Flemish
botanist De l'Obel at Silbury, between London
and Bath.
    As indicated by its name, used for curing
quinsy, an inflammation of the throat and
suppuration of the tonsils. Also used as an
astringent gargle.

TOOTHWORT

CORPSE FLOWER

Height 7–22cm/3–9in ☀ March–May

Lathraea squamaria
L *squamaria*, scaly

A creamy pink parasitic perennial that grows
on the roots of shrubs and trees, usually hazel
or elm. Its creeping base consists of creamy
oval scales or bracts that extend into a broad
clump. Short-stalked pink flowers and cream
bracts ascend up one side of a drooping stem.
Flowers are 2-lipped, held in a tube of hairy
sepals. Scales below each flower are modified
leaves resembling teeth and lacking
chlorophyll.
    Called Toothwort after its fang-like scales,
and Corpse Flower because of its deathly
appearance and because it was once believed
to spring from dead bodies. Gerard said
countrywomen called it Lungwort and used
it for coughs and lung infections.

VALERIAN

CAT'S LOVE (YORKSHIRE)

Height 15–80cm/6–32in   ☀ July–October

Valeriana officinalis
L *valere*, healthy; *officinalis*, medicinal

A perennial with a short conical rhizome.
Single erect stems are hairy near base. Lower
leaves pinnate with a terminal leaflet; upper
leaves unstalked, lance-shaped irregularly
toothed leaflets. Small pinkish-white flowers
in terminal umbrellas. Individual flowers
funnel-shaped, 5 lobed with 3 stamens.

Roots have a sedatory property, extract
used in many proprietary medicines and herbal
tranquillisers. A maceration of dried roots
used for headaches, nervous heart disorders
and insomnia. Valerian tea is common in
Germany to calm and prevent hysteria. No
side effects, but it can become addictive.
Cultivated in Derbyshire for medicinal use.

AGRIMONY, HEMP

ANDURION, HOLY ROPE

Height 30–120cm/12–48in ❀ July–September

Eupatorium cannabinum
After Eupator Mithridates VI, King of Pontus;
L *cannabinum*, like cannabis (the leaflets)

A tall downy perennial with a woody
rootstock. Round reddish downy furrowed
stem with few short branches, aromatic smell
when cut. Coarsely toothed leaves, leaflets
similar to cannabis, palmately lobed and
short-stalked, are borne in opposite pairs up
stem. Dense clusters of reddish flowers at end
of branches. Seeds have parachutes of white
hairs.

   Early herbalists used it for many cures – as a
purge, emetic, and for dropsy and jaundice. As
a poultice, or mixed with lard as an ointment,
it healed wounds. As an infusion it helped
colds and flu, but it was known as a 'rough'
medicine and had to be used with caution.

BURNET, SALAD

OLD MAN'S PEPPER, SOT HERB

Height 10–30cm/4–12in ❀ May–August

Sanguisorbia minor
L *sanguis*, blood; *sorbeo*, I absorb (stops
bleeding)
Burnet from Fr *burnete*, brunette

A short greyish tufted perennial. Leaves
mostly at base have 3–12 pairs of deeply
toothed roundish leaflets. Flowers are in dense
globular heads, red-styled female flowers on
top, yellow-stamened male flowers below with
green sepals and no petals. Smells of cucumber
when crushed.

   Herbal uses against diarrhoea, wounds
and internal bleeding. Fresh juice used for
tuberculosis. Once used as a spice for beer or
brandy. An infusion of leaves is believed to
cure a drunkard's thirst. Young leaves and
shoots are good in salads or as vegetables.

CRANESBILL, BLOODY

Height 10–30cm/4–12in ❀ June–August

Geranium sanguineum
Gk *geranos*, crane; L *sanguineum*, bloody
(the flowers)

A hairy spreading perennial with small leaves
deeply cut into 5–7 lobes. 5 reddish-purple
shallowly notched petals form each flower on
its individual branch. Cranesbill type fruit has
tuft at tip.

Medicinal use unknown but Gerard records
that the red flowers change to mulberry on the
second day, and on the third to a deep purple
tending to blueness. A pale pink or magenta
variety with purple-striped petals, Walney
Geranium (G. *sangineum* var. Lancastriense),
grows on the sand dunes on North Walney
Island where shells afford its necessary calcium
(see Vol. 2, Waterside Ways).

CRANESBILL, WOOD

MOUNTAIN FLOWER, THUNDER FLOWER,
KING'S HOOD

Height 30–50cm/12–20in ❀ June–July

Geranium sylvaticum
Gk *geranos*, crane; L *sylvaticum*, woodland

A hairy perennial with erect stems bearing
deeply lobed long-stalked leaves, similar to but
smaller than Meadow Cranesbill. 5 unnotched
reddish-purple flowers, often with a whitish
centre, borne on upright stalks. Typical
Cranesbill seed heads pointing upwards. A
northern species found from the Lakes and
Dales northwards. A hay meadow plant now
in decline because of the use of fertilisers and
modern silage methods, but still found in
damp woods and on roadsides.

No medical use known but superstition
said that to pick its flowers would bring on
thunderstorms.

HELLEBORINE, BROAD-LEAVED

COMMON HELLEBORINE

Height 25–75cm/10–30in ❀ July–September

Epipactis helleborine
Gk *epipactis*, named by Theophrastus;
helleborine, of the Hellebore family
Formerly *Helleborine latifolia* (broad-leaved)

An orchid with a short, thick, upward-growing
rootstock. Stems up to 61cm/24in covered
with short hairs – green above, purplish below.
Bears 4–10 pointed, oval-elliptic leaves
arranged spirally up the stem. 15–20 flowers
appear 8–9 years after germination, loosely
arranged on one side only of a spike, each
flower with 5 pointed sepals, green-tinged
with purple streaks. Petals pinkish-red with a
large lip, dark red inside, tip oval and curved
over, greenish-white or purple. Flowering
plant often surrounded by small sterile shoots.
Pollinated by insects. Common from midlands
southwards on both acid and alkaline soils, but
not rare in Cumbria.

HELLEBORINE, DARK RED

Height 23–45cm/9–18in ❀ July–August

Epipactis atro-rubens
Gk *epipactis*, named by Theophrastus;
L *atro*, dark; *rubens*, red

A rare orchid found only on limestone rocks
or screes. Its short thick root produces a leafy
stem from which many long thin roots extend
in all directions. Short downy stem has 5–10
leaves alternately in two opposing ranks, oval
to lanceolate, folded, dark green with reddish
tinge below. A stiff spike bears up to 36 small
deep red flowers with rough bosses on the lip.
Ovary very downy. Depends on cross-
pollination, with some reproduction from
roots. Most plants grow from seed.
    Epipactis is a genus in which the flower lip
stands out at right-angles from the column,
the lower part forming a basin-like hollow.
Found on screes and pavements in South
Lakeland and upper Eden valley. Rare.

BELLFLOWER, CREEPING

THROATWORT

Height 60–90cm/24–36in ❀ July–September

Campanula rapunculoides
L *campana*, bell; *rapunculoides*, similar to an
eastern bellflower

A tall slender perennial with underground
creeping runners that form large patches,
often in hedge banks. Toothed stalked oval
lower leaves; upper leaves narrower and
unstalked. Pale blue-violet flowers with
pointed hair-fringed petals hang down with
small bracts one side of an upright spike.
Lower flowers open first. Globular fruit
capsule. Introduced and naturalised from
Europe. Very common in Dentdale.

The doctrine of signatures suggested that
throat-like flowers would help sore throats.
Contains an acrid milky juice, but is not
poisonous. Young leaves and shoots can
be cooked as a green vegetable.

BLUEBELL

HYACINTH, SQUILL,
CROWFOOT (CUMBERLAND), CROWTOES

Height 20–50cm/8–20in ❀ April–June

Scilla non-scripta or *Hyacinthoides non-scripta*
Gk *scilla*, name for Sea Squill; L *non-scripta*,
unrecorded (i.e. by Greeks and Romans in
Western Europe)

White bulb gives rise to narrowish strap-like
leaves. Flowers on a drooping one-sided spike,
blue, bell-shaped, honey-scented. Fruit capsule
splits into 6 segments to disperse black seeds.
Bulbs do not multiply. Plants can be destroyed
by trampling. A relatively rare woodland plant
of Western Europe, rapidly becoming rare
worldwide.

Bulbs contain starch used in Elizabethan
times to stiffen ruffs and cuffs. Also used to
make glue. Considered unlucky to bring into
houses. Named by Homer after Hyacinthus, a
Spartan youth loved and accidentally killed by
Apollo; from his blood sprang a purple flower.

BUGLE

THUNDER AND LIGHTNING

Height 8–30cm/3–12in ☀ May–July

Ajuga repens
L *abigo*, to drive away (disease); *repens*,
creeping
Bugle from L *bugulus*, young bull (plant was
known to apothecaries as Bugula)

A woodland perennial with creeping woody
runners. Has a rosette of long-stalked ovate
leaves, purple beneath. Unstemmed stalk
leaves opposite, often purplish, up a stiff stem.
Pale blue flowers in whorls above stem leaves.
Short upper lip exposes blue stamens. Fruit is a
short bell-shaped tube containing 4 nutlets.
   Medieval herbalists grew it widely as a cure-
all. Culpeper advised a syrup of Bugle for
'wounds, thrusts and stabs, ulcers and broken
bones'. Recommended for delirium tremens.
Still in use, infusion of Bugle and Peppermint
taken for dyspepsia and gall disorders.

COLUMBINE

GRANNY'S BONNET, FOOL'S CAP

Height 30–80cm/12–32in ☀ June–July

Aquilegia vulgaris
From L *aquila*, eagle (petal shape)
Columbine from L *columba*, dove (petal shape)

Perennial with a stout branched stock.
Hairless erect stems bear slightly greyish
leaves, 3-lobed on fine stalks. Blue,
occasionally white, drooping flowers have
5 sepals and 5 petals each with a long curved
spur making them resemble 5 perched pigeons.
Scented like hay. Hairy fruit erect like a
cluster of 5 pea pods. Seeds are dispersed
nearby creating small colonies.
   Leaves once made into poultices. Infusions
for liver and gall bladder disorders, skin
irritations including scurvy, and jaundice.
Rubbed on the hands, it was believed in
medieval times to give one the courage of
lions. One of the badges of the House of
Lancaster and the Earls of Derby.

GENTIAN, SPRING

Height 2.5–15cm/1–6in ❀ April–June

Gentiana verna
After Gentius, King of Illyria, who used it
medicinally; L *verna*, spring-flowering

A rare hairless perennial with underground
creeping roots giving rise to rosettes of oval
leaves. Short erect stems with a few small
lance-shaped leaves bear single flowers, blue-
green outside, blue inside, with a white stigma
in a narrow tube with wide-spreading lobes.
Fruits are seeds, seldom sown, being eaten by
sheep before they can disperse. Vegetative
propagation by stolons. Found in British Isles
only in Teesdale at 366m/1,200ft and higher,
and in the Burren, Ireland. Also in Europe,
Alps, Pyrenees, Balkans and across highland
Asia.

In Germany it is a thunder plant; pick it
and storms follow.

HAREBELL

SCOTTISH BLUEBELL, WITCHES' THIMBLES,
FAIRY BELLS

Height 15–40cm/6–16in ❀ July–September

Campanula rotundifolia
L *campana*, bell; *rotundifolia*, round-leaved

A perennial with a creeping underground
stolon producing unbranched slender erect
stems. Basal leaves round or heart-shaped on
short stalks. Upper leaves unstalked, lance-
shaped. Hanging blue flowers bell-shaped.
Fruit capsule releases a few seeds at a time
from basal pores. The round leaves at the
base wither before the flowers come out.

In parts of Scotland and in the song, these
are the 'Blue Bells of Scotland' (where the
English Bluebell is called Hyacinth). Also
called the Old Man's Bell, the Devil's Bell and
Witch Bell (the hare is also a witch animal in
folk myth). The family badge of the
McDonalds.

IVY, GROUND

ALEHOOF, GILL

Height 10–60cm/4–24in ☀ April–July

Glechoma hederacea
Gk *glechom*, mint; L *hederacea*, ivy-like

A creeping perennial with erect flowering
stems. Long-stalked opposite kidney-shaped
bluntly toothed leaves grow on both creeping
and flowering stems. Slightly aromatic.
Flowers in whorls of 2–4 up stem all face same
way, violet-blue, 2 notched lips on straight
tube. Fruits 4 nutlets.

Astringent, diuretic. Infusions used for
piles, coughs, catarrh and abdominal disorders.
A gargle for mouth and throat infections, a
tonic and vermifuge. Before the introduction
of hops in in the 16th century it was used for
flavouring beer, hence the name Alehoof.
Young shoots and leaves can be added to
soup or cooked like spinach.

MILKWORT

ROGATION FLOWER

Height 5–10cm/2–4in ☀ May–September

Polygala vulgaris
Gk *poly*, much; *gala*, milk; L *vulgaris*, common

A perennial with a woody root stock.
No rosette but upright slender stems bear
alternate oval to elliptic leaves. The flowers
have 3 tiny green sepals and 2 big bluish
inner sepals cradling the tube of 5 petals fused
together. The lowest petal is fringed. Flowers
can be blue, white or pink.

Flowers considered to resemble udders,
therefore infusions were believed to increase
mothers' milk. A valuable ingredient in
herbal medicines for respiratory problems,
also used as an expectorant and cough cure.
In Guernsey it is used to cure paralysis and
strokes. If it flowered in time, it was carried
in Rogation Week ceremonies on 20 May.

SCABIOUS, SMALL

LESSER SCABIOUS

Height 15–70cm/6–28in ❀ July–October

Scabiosa columbaria
L *scabies*, a form of leprosy (cure for);
columbaria, dove-like

A many-branched hairy perennial. Upright
stems have toothed oval leaves at base. Upper
leaves finely cut, almost stalkless. Single
flower heads, flatter than Field Scabious
(*Knautia arvensis*; *Waterside Ways*, page 95),
consist of a cluster of blue-lilac florets, outer
ones only with 5 large petals. Fruits are scaly
cups with 5 sepals projected. Seeds dispersed
by wind. Found in limestone or chalky soils.

As its name implies, it was once thought
to cure skin troubles, wounds, sores, dandruff
and freckles. It was also used for purifying the
blood. The root is no longer used in herbal
medicine.

SPEEDWELL, GERMANDER

BONNY BIRD'S EYE

Height 10–30cm/4–12in ❀ April–July

Veronica chamaedrys
After St Veronica, believed to have wiped
Christ's face with it, or from Gk *phero*, I bring;
nike, *victory*; L *chamaedrys*, creeping
Speedwell from its fast cure; Gk *germander*,
on the ground

A slim hairy perennial with hairs in 2 opposite
lines down stems, often prostrate at base.
Leaves dark green, coarsely toothed. Brilliant
sky-blue flowers with white centres borne in
stalked bunches at base of leaves. Hairy heart-
shaped capsule cradles seeds.

Astringent, once used to purify the blood.
In Ireland, boiled in milk for jaundice; in
Guernsey, taken as tea for indigestion and
stomach pains. However, it has little
medicinal value.

VIOLET, DOG

Height 2.5–20cm/1–8in ✸ April–July

Viola riviniana
L *viola*, plant family name
Dog from its inferiority to other varieties
(cf Dog Rose, Dog's Mercury, Dogwood)

A low hairy perennial with long slightly hairy straggling stems. Heart-shaped leaves as broad as long and with serrated edges borne on long stalks. Scentless deep blue-violet flowers with a stout paler spur, often upcurved and notched or furrowed at tip. Pointed sepals. Fruit a triangular 3-valved seed capsule.

Dog Violet is cathartic and emetic, but not much used now. An infusion of violet can be used for headaches. Gypsies make a poultice from the leaves against cancers. Sweet Violet, but not Dog Violet, is used in cooking, medicine and decoration.

ORCHID, BIRD'S NEST

Height up to 30cm/12in ☀ May–July

Neottia nidis-avis
neottia, name of an Eastern orchid family;
L *nidis*, nest; *avis*, bird

Yellowish-brown fruiting spikes rise singly,
without leaves, directly from an untidy clump
of stubby subterranean velvet-covered roots
that give rise to the name Bird's Nest; these
feed on mycorhizal fungus. The lower part of
the erect leafless stems are clad with lance-
shaped sheaths, with many brownish-yellow
orchid-type flowers, rather like those of the
Twayblade, the sepals and petals forming an
open hood at the back, with a large two-lipped
lobe hanging at the front. Bright yellow
pollen-carriers (pollinia) highlight the centre.
Grows in heavily shaded woodland, usually
beech, with a deep moist leaf litter over a
lime-rich soil. From germination the rhizomes
take 9 years to acquire enough food to develop
an aerial flower-bearing stem.

ORCHID, FLY

Height 15–45cm/6–18in ☀ May–June

Ophrys insectifera
Gk *ophrys*, orchid; *insectifera*, insect-bearing

First leaf appears a year after germination,
followed by first tuber. Aerial shoot increases
in height over several years before its
flowering spike develops. 3 or 4 leaves support
an upright stem that can bear up to 8 widely
spaced flowers. 3 blunt greenish sepals cradle
2 narrow brown petals (antennae), the narrow
lip is reddish-brown, cleft at the tip with a
metallic band across the centre (the fly's
body). An easily overlooked orchid,
resembling a blade of grass with a perched fly.
Prefers shady grassy places or ash woodland on
limestone. It is found in South Lakeland and
on limestone crags in the upper Eden valley,
its northern limit.

The eleven ferns described on the following pages can be encountered on the walks
in this book. Their attractive fronds of varying shapes and shades compensate for the
lack of colourful flowers. They reproduce by wind dispersal of the spores produced on
the backs of the fronds. These are retained until ripe in capsules (sporangia) which
cluster together in circular, linear or horse-shoe groups (sori). The spores germinate
in moist ground and develop after about 12 weeks into tiny fan-shaped plants like
baby Liverworts, called prothalli. These produce sperm from the undersides and an
egg cell on the upper. The embryo fern develops on the prothallus until it becomes
self-supporting, initially below the soil to form a rhizome. Thence it develops into a
baby fern. Some ferns grow only on limy soil, and the Rigid Buckler and Maidenhair
Ferns are rare even there.

FERN, RIGID BUCKLER

Height 20–60cm/8–24in ☀ July–August

Dryopteris villarsii
Gk *drys*, oak; *pteris*, fern; L *submontana*, below
mountains
Buckler, a small round shield

A very rare deciduous fern found in limestone
cracks and crevices only in NW England and
North Wales. A blackish stock retains decayed
ends of fronds. Fronds erect or spreading
covered in short yellowish hairs. Stalk half as
long as blade, with brown scales at base. Up to
25 pinnae on each side of blade, with rounded
toothed lobes. Large round sori in 2 rows up
each fertile pinnule. When crushed the fronds
emit a fragrance like hay or balsam. Most
likely to be seen on South Lakeland limestone
rocks and pavements. Found from the Alps to
the Pyrenees in Europe.

FERN, HART'S TONGUE

Height up to 60cm/up to 24in July–August

Phyllitis scolopendrium
Gk *phyllon*, leaf; *scolopendra*, millipede

A perennial evergreen fern with a dense scaly
rhizome. Fronds rise in tufts. Blades have short
stalks covered with brown scales, heart-shaped
base, strap-shaped tapering to a point and,
unlike any other fern, undivided with parallel
veins. Spore cases (sori) in diagonal lines
across undersides are like brown millipedes.

   Used for over 2,000 years to treat diarrhoea
and dysentery. Used underside up for scalds
and burns and for erysipalis. Legend says it
was a pillow for Jesus who left two hairs in
its stem. Can you spot them?

FERN, LIMESTONE

LIMESTONE POLYPODY

Height up to 22cm/up to 9in ☀ July–August

Gymnocarpium robertianum
Gk *gymnos*, naked; *karpos*, fruit (no indusium
over sori); L *robertianum*, resembling *Geranium*
robertianum

A delicate deciduous fern with a creeping root
stock from which rise, singly, mealy-looking
dull green fronds (minute glandular hairs
below, as in Rigid Buckler Fern). When
crushed the fronds exude a sweet apple-like
scent. Sori are in uncovered clusters near the
margins of the leaflets. Found only in
Cumbrian and Yorkshire Dales limestone areas
up to about 245m/800ft. Becoming quite rare.
Sometimes called the Limestone Oak Fern, as
it resembles Oak Fern (G. *dryopteris*) which
grows in damp woods and on high rock ledges
in Lakeland.

FERN, MAIDENHAIR

Height up to 30cm/12in ☀ June–September

Adiantum capillus-veneris
Gk *adiantos*, unwetted (repels water);
L *capillus*, hair; *veneris*, of Venus (delicate
foliage)

Normally evergreen but dies back in this area.
A delicate perennial with a creeping rhizome,
in Northern England usually found on tufa
or moist rocks near sea. Leaves up to about
15cm/6in long with branched, black wiry
stalks. Fan-shaped leaflets are toothed at the
tips with no midrib, veins forking to ends.
Semi-circular sori in inrolled ends of leaflets.
Very rare.
    Whole plant has been used as an infusion
to stimulate menstruation and against coughs
and bronchitis. Gerard says: 'It consumeth and
wasteth away the King's Evil and other hard
swellings, and it maketh the haire of the head
or beard to grow that is fallen and pulled off.'

FERN, MALE

Height 30–150cm/12–60 in ✷ Deciduous

Dryopteris filix-mas
Gk *drys*, oak; *pteris*, fern; *filix-mas*, male fern

A stout woody stock with tenacious wiry root hairs holds a number of closely packed crowns. Fronds, arranged in shuttlecock form, have stalks ⅛–⅓ length of the lance-shaped mid-green blades. 20–50 flat serrated pinnules arranged alternately on each side of the rachi (blade stalk) are rounded at the ends with kidney-shaped sori in two lines on the undersides.

In classical times an oil was extracted from its roots as a vermifuge, a practice commended by Gerard. Later herbalists claimed that the roots boiled in lard made a good ointment for healing wounds. As with bracken, its fronds were burnt to make glass and soap. The common name dates back to before the Middle Ages when all plants were believed to be male or female.

FERN, GOLDEN MALE

SCALY MALE FERN

Height 30–150cm/12–60in ✷ Semi-wintergreen

Dryopteris afinis
Gk *drys*, oak; *pteris*, fern; L *afinis*, related to (the Male Fern)

Similar in many ways to *D. filix-mas* but the stalk and rachis are covered with bright orange-yellow scales that turn brown when mature. Its fronds are a lighter green and the pinnae have a dark brown patch near the base. When they unfurl in spring, the croziers are a bright golden green clothed with golden scales. Less common than *D. filix-mas*, this fern prefers woodlands and upland becksides to the more open and unshaded valleys and fells of its ubiquitous relation. The two species often hybridise.

Qualities and uses identical to *D. filix-mas*.

FERN, RUSTY-BACK

RUSTY-BACK, COMMON SPLEENWORT,
MILTWASTE (MILT = SPLEEN), SCALY FERN

Height 5–20cm/2–8in ✳ April–October

Ceterach officinarum
Arabic *ceterach*, plant name; L *officinarum*,
of herbal use

A distinctive small wintergreen fern that
grows on limestone or in mortar. Short
brown stems support each frond with alternate
ovate segments rather like a skewed ladder,
increasing in size upwards, with a few scales
above and densely packed tile-like silvery
scales below hiding lines of spore cases.
With age the scales become rust-coloured.
In drought, the whole plant shrivels up but
soon recovers when rain comes.

   Once used as a herbal remedy for
conditions of the spleen and liver, and
removing urinary crystals. Pliny considered
its use would cause women to become barren.

MOONWORT

Height 2–15cm/1–6in ✳ Deciduous

Botrychium lunaria
Gk *botry*, bunched; L *lunatus*, with little
crescent moons

A short perennial fern rising from an upright
stock. It produces only two fronds each
year, one male, one female. One is leaf-like
consisting of 5 or 7 moon-shaped leaflets on
a long stalk; yhe other rising from the base
is 2-pinnate, bearing clusters of yellow spore
cases, taller than the first. Numerous along the
track to Cauldron Snout in late May and June
(see Walk 16).

   Culpeper says it was used for wounds,
bruises, fractures, ruptures and bleeding.
Gerard tells us that the key-like fronds will
open locks and remove the shoes from horses
passing over them. Believed in medieval times
to be gathered by witches in moonlight and
used in their incantations.

SPLEENWORT, GREEN

WINTERGREEN

Height 5–15cm/2–6in ☀ June–September

Asplenium viride
Gk *a*, not; *splen*, spleen (medical use);
L *viride*, green

A dwarf tufted wall fern with a creeping
brown stock and fronds of bright green with
green stalks up to 15cm/6in long. The fronds
hang softly, not bristly like Maidenhair
Spleenwort, and have up to 30 pairs of
toothed rounded fan-shaped leaflets. It has
green midribs. Its sori are set in lines along
the leaflet veins. It only grows in rocks and
walls with a high limestone content. To be
seen especially in crevices on cliffs at western
side of Watlowes Dry Valley near Malham
(Walk 10), and many limestone scars above
250m/820ft in the Dales. Common in
E. Cumbria but rare in S. Cumbria.
  Pharmaceutical uses, if any, are obscure.

SPLEENWORT, MAIDENHAIR

WINTERGREEN

Height 5–20cm/2–8in ☀ May–October

Asplenium trichomanes
Gk *a*, not; *splen*, spleen (medicinal use);
tricho, hair
Maidenhair perhaps from black stalks after
leaflets have fallen

A small tufted fern with a woody stock and
narrow shiny leaves with long, opposite
leaflets oval and slightly toothed on a blackish
stalk. Spore cases are in short oblique lines
under the leaflets. Common on rocks or in
crevices; ground-hugging.
  Name suggests herbal use for spleen
disorders. Culpeper also says it is useful
against jaundice and hiccoughs. Tea made
from the fronds, sweet, sticky and expectorant,
was once considered useful for pulmonary
complaints, and is used on Arran as a laxative.

WALL RUE

WINTERGREEN, TENTWORT

Height 5–7.5cm/2–3in ☀ June–October

Asplenium ruta-muraria
Gk *a*, not; *splen*, spleen (medicinal); *ruta*, rue;
L *muralis*, on walls

A small tufted fern rising from a short
creeping branching stock, the younger parts
covered in black scales with hair-like points.
Fronds 2–15cm/1–6in long, stalks twice as
long as blades, dark purple-brown at base with
scale-like hairs, upper parts green or greyish.
Blade triangular with 4 or 5 alternate
roundish, toothed or fan-shaped secondary
leaflets. Spore cases in lines along leaflets
merge together when ripe.

Once used as herbal cure for the 'taint'
(rickets), hence its name Tentwort. Culpeper
recommended it for coughs, shortness of
breath, jaundice, diseases of the spleen and
urinary infections. He also praised its value as
a hair restorer and a cure for scalp conditions.

Opposite: Melancholy Thistle (*Cirsium
helenoides*; page 73) at Swaledale, Walk 13

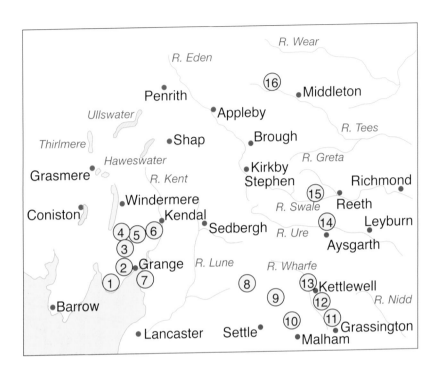

SYMBOLS USED IN THE MAPS

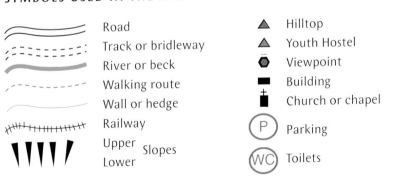

Road
Track or bridleway
River or beck
Walking route
Wall or hedge
Railway
Upper
Lower Slopes

Hilltop
Youth Hostel
Viewpoint
Building
Church or chapel
P Parking
WC Toilets

WALKS

		km	miles	hours
1	HUMPHREY HEAD	3.25	2	$1^1/_2$
2	HAMPSFELL	5.5	$3^1/_2$	$2-2^1/_2$
3	LATTERBARROW & WINSTER VALLEY	13	8	4–5
4	WHITBARROW WEST	9	$5^1/_2$	3–4
5	WHITBARROW EAST	11.5	$7^1/_2$	$3^1/_2-4^1/_2$
6	SCOUT SCAR	10	$6^1/_4$	$3-3^1/_2$
7	ARNSIDE	10	$6^1/_4$	$3^1/_2-4^1/_2$
8A	INGLEBOROUGH	11.5	$7^1/_2$	$4-4^1/_2$
8B	INGLEBOROUGH	10	$6^1/_4$	$3^1/_2-4^1/_2$
9	PEN Y GHENT	9.5	6	$4-4^1/_2$
10	MALHAM	9.5	6	$3^1/_2-4$
11	GRASS WOOD & CONISTON DIB	13	8	$4-4^1/_2$
12	KETTLEWELL SOUTH	14	9	$4^1/_2-5^1/_2$
13	KETTLEWELL NORTH	8	5	3–4
14	CARPERBY & AYSGARTH FALLS	9	$5^1/_2$	$3^1/_2-4^1/_2$
15	GUNNERSIDE	8	5	$3-3^1/_2$
16	WIDDYBANK FELL, UPPER TEESDALE	13.5	$8^1/_4$	4–5

INTRODUCTION

The walks have been carefully selected to take you through the most interesting botanical areas, to make each one a floristic experience. In some cases they will reveal carpets of prolific colonies, in others the opportunity to see often isolated species of very rare flowers. With the aid of the Directory pictures and descriptions, the flowering charts and the list of what species to look out for, discovery and recognition should not be difficult. All the walks are on public or permitted footpaths and with one exception (Purple Saxifrage on Walks 8 and 9) the flowers have been located within two metres of the paths, so any trespass away from the paths is inexcusable.

The second criterion in choosing the walks has been their own intrinsic qualities, particularly in terms of landscape. Each is a classic walk in its own right.

The maps have been drawn to show only relevant landmarks and features, even down to field walls (thin black lines) in cases where finding the route might be difficult. Walking routes are indicated by dotted red lines, with red arrows to indicate preferred directions, but since all walks are circular they can be taken in the opposite direction, depending on weather conditions. Exposed upland paths, for example, should be done with a following wind, while strong headwinds need to be countered by sheltered valley or woodland paths.

Most would be classified as easy, and the times given assume a gentle pace of two miles per hour with adequate stopping time for identification and photography. All involve some measure of climbing, but seldom steeply. Each is well within the compass of any reasonably fit person under the age of ninety.

Because of occasional gravelly descents, well-cleated boots or shoes are recommended. Wellingtons can be used, but they tend to slip on wet limestone rocks.

In 1997 the Ordnance Survey issued a new series (NS) of Outdoor Leisure Maps that considerably extended the boundaries of the old series (OS). References are given to both.

Opposite: Daffodil (*Narcissus pseudonarcissus*;
page 38) at Glencoyne shore, Ullswater

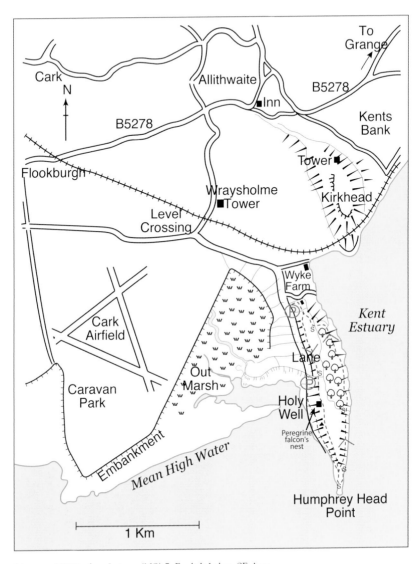

Map: use OS Outdoor Leisure (NS) 7, English Lakes, SE Area
or OS Pathfinder 636, Grange over Sands

WALK 1 ◆ HUMPHREY HEAD

Distance 3.25 km / 2 miles
Time 1½ hours

To get there, take the B5278 from
Grange over Sands west towards
Flookburgh. Just beyond Allithwaite
and Guide over Sands pub on left, go
L along side road signed Humphrey
Head and Holy Well. After level
crossing go L at T-junction, then park
beside drive up to the Outdoor Centre
where there is a display board for
Humphrey Head (SD388747). Walk up
drive, turning R beyond pole to follow
West cliff edge past Trig point to stile
at extreme South tip. Stile gives access
to shore which can be followed for a
short distance northwards to another
stile back into the nature reserve.
Alternatively, continue along
peninsular edge above low cliffs to stile
into wood. About 100m in, take L fork
to end of wood, then L up to stile into
pasture. Follow back to start.

While many interesting flowers are
seen on this walk, the greatest variety
of plants exists on the cliffs. By driving
down to the foreshore where cars may
be parked, a short walk southwards
gives access to the lower cliff levels
which are well worth exploring. Bird
watchers will delight in this area, and
in walking around the embankment
round Cark Airfield, a parachute
training base.

LOOK OUT FOR

Rock-Rose, Green Winged Orchid,
Squinancywort, Wood Anemone,
Yarrow, Enchanter's Nightshade,
Dropwort, Dog Violet, Hoary
Rock-Rose, Dove's Foot Cranesbill,
Tormentil, Pignut, Betony, Deadly
Nightshade, Small Scabious

In the wood
Golden Rod, Figwort, Herb Bennet,
Centaury

Shore birds include Common,
Black-Headed and Lesser Black-
Backed Gulls, Oystercatchers,
Curlews and Dunlin.
Ducks include Shelduck and
Pintail.
Green and Spotted Woodpeckers
on the Head.

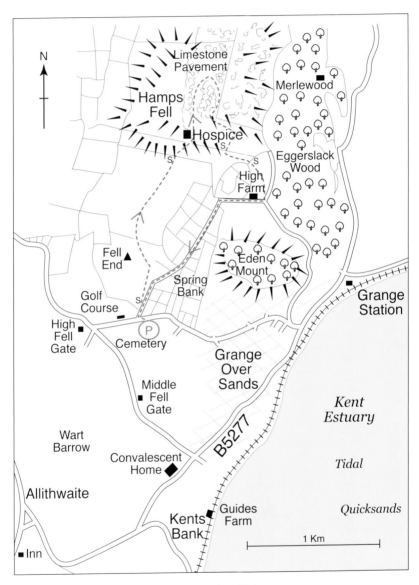

N

Limestone
Pavement

Hamps
Fell

Merlewood

Hospice

S

Eggerslack
Wood

High
Farm

Fell
End

Spring
Bank

Eden
Mount

Golf
Course

S

Grange
Station

High
Fell
Gate

Cemetery

P

Grange
Over
Sands

Middle
Fell
Gate

Kent
Estuary

Wart
Barrow

Tidal

Allithwaite

Convalescent
Home

B5277

Kents
Bank

Guides
Farm

Quicksands

Inn

1 Km

Map: use OS Outdoor Leisure (NS) 7, English Lakes, SE Area
or OS Pathfinder 636, Grange over Sands

WALK 2 ◆ HAMPSFELL

Distance 5.5 km / 3½ miles
Time 2–2½ hours

To get there leave the A590(T) at Meathop roundabout, and follow B5278 to Grange. At roundabout at top of hill, go R up Grange Fell on the road towards Cartmel. Park on wide roadside verge (SD 396778) near Grange Fell Golf Course. Walk up Spring Bank Lane opposite for 100m. Over stile on L strike diagonally R up hillside, and straight on along a clear path up to Hospice on Hampsfield Fell where there is a viewpoint. Landowner permits exploration of the limestone pavement, with many rare species in grykes. Return ESE from Hospice on path skirting wall corner. After a short scrambly descent through rocks clad in Squinancywort, take upper of two paths, contouring round to a stile. Cross and descend diagonally to another stile. Over here, descend through herb-rich meadow to farm road. Go R along road past High Farm and Spring Bank back to start.

From the Hospice, panoramic view embraces Black Combe towards the W; Dow Crag and Coniston Old Man with Scafell between them to the NW; the Langdale Pikes, Skiddaw and the

LOOK OUT FOR

May	Spring Sandwort, Orchids
June	Squinancywort, Mouse-Ear Hawkweed, Whitlow Grass
July	Golden Rod, Broad-Leaved Helleborine, Pignut
August	Angular Solomon's Seal, Lesser Meadow Rue
September	Ploughman's Spikenard, Burnet Saxifrage

Helvellyn Range to the N; the Ill Bell Ridge and Kentmere Fells E of N. Towards the E are the Howgill Fells, then two of North Yorkshire's Three Peaks: Whernside and Ingleborough. Across the estuary, the Bowland Fells back the large buildings of Lancaster, and beyond Morecambe the ugly blocks of Heysham Nuclear Power Station intrude. In the bay you may spot gas and oil platforms.

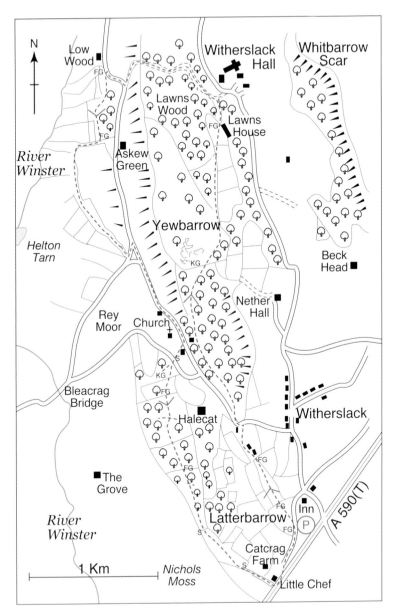

Map: use OS Outdoor Leisure (NS) 7, English Lakes SE Area *or* OS Pathfinder 627, Levens

WALK 3
LATTERBARROW & WINSTER VALLEY

Distance 13 km / 8 miles
Time 4–5 hours
Easy going all the way

To get there, drive along A590(T).
At turn-off signed Witherslack, 1.5 km
NE of Grange roundabout, proceed to
Derby Arms Inn, and turn L along
disued A590 to a bridleway on R
signed High Fell (SD 441827). Park
here. Walk up bridleway through
Latterbarrow Nature Reserve, keeping
to the track, and follow it through
fields to High Fell End. At road go L
for 60m then follow bridleway through
woods to Yewbarrow and track above
Witherslack Hall. Turn L along this
track through woods to descend to road
in Winster Valley. Go R along road for
300m, then take footpath on L across a
field to a lane. Go R down the lane for
150m, then L alongside hedge. 1km on,
at a minor road, go L to join valley
road. Turn R past old quarry to church,
follow footpath to R that winds below
Old Vicarage, then L at fork through
Halecat Woods. Keep straight ahead,
ignoring side paths to end of woods,
then across fields and over stile to pass
Catcrag Farm to A590(T). Go L past
Little Chef to join old A590 on L back
to start.

LOOK OUT FOR

February	Snowdrops, Golden Saxifrage
March	Daffodil, Primrose, Whitlow Grass
April	Spring Sandwort, Bluebell, Early Purple Orchid
May	Butterfly Orchid, Rock-Rose, Columbine
June	Squinancywort, Milkwort, Twayblade
July	Fragrant and Spotted Orchid, Burnet Saxifrage
August	Ploughman's Spikenard, Harebell, Angular Solomon's Seal
September	Felwort, Small Scabious, Burnet Saxifrage

Listen out for Greater Spotted and
Green Woodpecker, Woodlark,
Nuthatch and Jay in woods;
elsewhere Little and Tawny Owl,
Swallow, Chiffchaff, Willow
Warbler, Blackcap, Treecreeper,
Tits and Wren. You may see Red
Squirrel and Roe Deer.

A permit to go off the track in Latterbarrow Nature Reserve can be booked in advance from
Cumbria Wildlife Trust, Plumgarths, Crook Road, Kendal LA8 0LF.

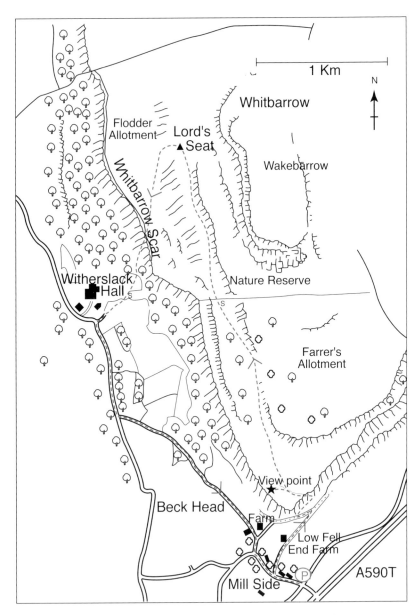

Map: use OS Outdoor Leisure (NS) 7, English Lakes SE Area *or* OS Pathfinder 627, Levens

WALK 4 ◆ WHITBARROW WEST

Distance 9 km / 5½ miles
Time 3–4 hours
Boots or strong shoes recommended

To get there, take A590(T). Between
B5277, Grange roundabout and A5074,
Bowness Road, side road to N signed
Mill Side and Beck Head leads to old
A590 and wide verge for parking
(SD 452840). Walk 200m towards
Mill Side. Turn R along bridleway past
Low Fell End Farm to track below scar
wood. Go L along track for 60m, then
R up hill following white arrows
(permissive path). At first wall, where
path does a dog-leg R, divert straight
ahead for 60m to viewpoint. Here look
out for Hoary and Common Rock-Rose,
Wood Sage, Small Scabious and others.
Return to wall and follow well-trodden,
cairned path to Hervey memorial cairn
on Lord's Seat with panoramic views.
Turn L (W) and follow path through
Flodder Allotment to stile in wall at top
of scar wood. Follow steep, stony path
down to join lane at Witherslack Hall
(SD 437860). Continue on to road,
and go L for 700m, then L along public
bridleway and road to Beck Head, and
back to start.

Witherslack Hall was once the hunting lodge
of Lord Stanley, Earl of Derby, hence Lord's
Seat. Previous owners included John Barwick,
a royalist spy rewarded with the Deanship of
St Paul's. His brother Peter was physician to
King Charles II.

LOOK OUT FOR

March	Whitlow Grass, Wood Sorrel, Barren Strawberry
April	Early Purple Orchid, Lesser Celandine, Woodruff
May	Wall Lettuce, Wild Strawberry, Rue-Leaved Saxifrage
June	Hoary and Common Rock-Rose, Thyme
July	Ground Ivy, Squinancywort, Small Scabious
August	Broad-leaved and Dark Red Helleborine, Eyebright
September	Felwort, Hemp Agrimony, Harebell

See if you can identify Bird Cherry,
Spindle Tree, Rowan, Lancastrian
Whitebeam, Ash, Small-leaved
Lime.
Birds (seen or heard) should include
Buzzard, Raven, Crow, Blackbird,
Thrush, Meadow Pipit, Skylark,
Willow Warbler, Chiffchaff,
Swallow, Great Spotted and Green
Woodpeckers, Chaffinch, Blue,
Great, Coal and Long-Tailed Tits,
Cuckoo, Wood Pigeons.

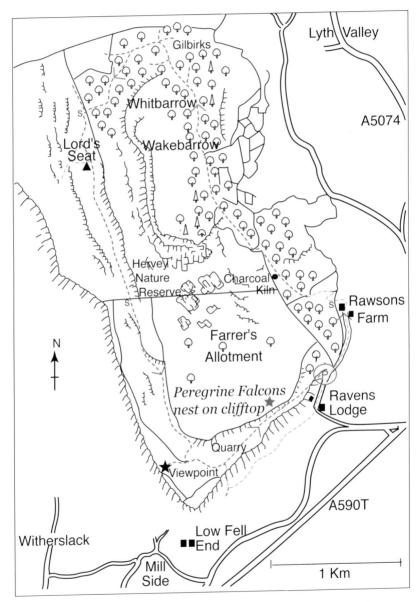

Map: use OS Outdoor Leisure (NS) 7, English Lakes SE Area *or* OS Pathfinder 627, Levens

WALK 5 ◆ WHITBARROW EAST

Distance 11.5 km / 7½ miles
Time 3½–4½ hours

To get there take A590(T) between
Grange and Levens Bridge. At the first
minor road W of A5074, Bowness
Road, turn along old A590 forking R
up to Raven's Lodge. Go R behind farm
and park clear of track (SD 461853).
Walk along to Rawsons Farm.
Immediately past farm go L through
stile into wood. On reaching track, go
R, past a charcoal furnace, then 200m
on take footpath to L and follow yellow
arrows. At a fork below large old oak
trees keep R until next path on L with
a yellow arrow. Follow path up to fell
wall. Cross stile and ascend L to Lord's
Seat. From here follow clear permissive
path (cairns then white arrows) down
to fell wall. Footpath does a dog-leg
to L, but a 50m diversion to R leads
to a fine viewpoint and more flowers.
Resume along white arrowed path to
T-junction. Here go L and over stile
to follow permissive path across quarry
level below Peregrine Falcons nest
down to start. Or go R to join track
near Whitbarrow Lodge and L to
Raven's Lodge and start.

LOOK OUT FOR

April	Wood Anemone, Primrose, Cowslip, Coltsfoot
May	Wood Sorrel, Woodruff, Early Purple Orchid
June	Tormentil, Rock-Rose, Hoary Rock-Rose
July	Spotted Orchid, Mouse-Ear Hawkweed, Bird's Foot Trefoil
August	Felwort, Betony, Small Scabious, Dropwort
September	Ploughman's Spikenard, Burnet Saxifrage, Hemp Agrimony
October	Carline Thistle, Yarrow, Golden Rod

You may see Roe Deer and young
in the woods in June, and Red
Squirrels and Rabbits at any time;
peregrine falcons may show noisy
disapproval if they have eggs or
chicks in their nest.

The Hervey Reserve is crossed by only one public footpath and one permissive path. Its 250
acres are worthy of exploration by permit, booked in advance from Cumbria Wildlife Trust,
Plumgarths, Crook Road, Kendal LA8 0LF. Annual membership at a very reasonable cost
covers a wide range of reserves in the county.

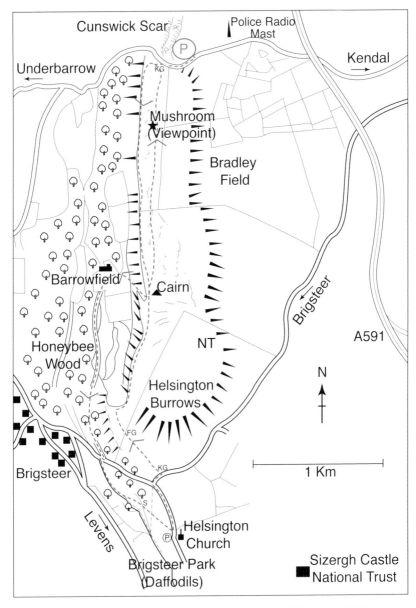

Map: use OS Outdoor Leisure (NS) 7, English Lakes SE Area *or* OS Pathfinder 627, Levens

WALK 6 ◆ SCOUT SCAR

Distance 10 km / 6¼ miles
Time 3–3½ hours
Easy walking, splendid views

Park at the National Park Car Park
(SD 488924) on the Kendal–
Underbarrow Road. Cross to gate
slightly to R along road. Follow clifftop
path past Mushroom viewpoint. After
2.5km go R at large cairn down through
scar wood to Barrowfield Farm. Follow
track to L through Honeybee Wood.
At Kendal–Brigsteer Road go R for
80m to join bridleway on L. After
500m, narrow footpath on L angles R
up through wood (in spring, carry on to
visit Brigsteer Woods with its oceans of
wild Daffodils). At stile, cross diagonally
half R over meadow towards clump of
trees and Helsington Church (note its
mural and leather altar frontal). Take
paved track L to road. Go R to gate
on L into Helsington Burrows (NT).
Follow distinct path back to scar edge.
Just beyond cairn, veer R to join a
higher track to Mushroom and back
to start.

Nearby Sizergh Castle (NT), home of the
Stricklands built round a pele tower, was often
visited by Queen Katherine Parr whose family
had owned Kendal castle and whose aunt
Agnes Parr was married to Sir Thomas
Strickland. Sizergh derives from Sigar's
erg, dairy farm.

LOOK OUT FOR

March	Daffodil, Coltsfoot, Primrose
April	Whitlow Grass, Spring Sandwort, Celandine
May	Common and Hoary Rock-Rose, Lily of the Valley
June	Spring Sandwort, Early Purple Orchid, Sweet Cicely
July	Limestone Bedstraw, Pignut, Squinancywort
August	Dropwort, Wild Basil, Burnet Saxifrage
September	Betony, Eyebright, Carline Thistle
October	Harebell, Golden Rod, Cat's Ear

Birds include Green and Great
Spotted Woodpecker, Song
Thrush, Blackbird, Nuthatch,
Chaffinch, Fieldfare (spring and
autumn), Blackcap, Robin, Raven,
Gulls, Blue Tit, Great Tit, Coal
Tit, Wood Pigeon, Kestrel,
Sparrowhawk, Merlin, Buzzard,
Wren, Cuckoo.
Roe Deer and Wood Mouse often
seen.

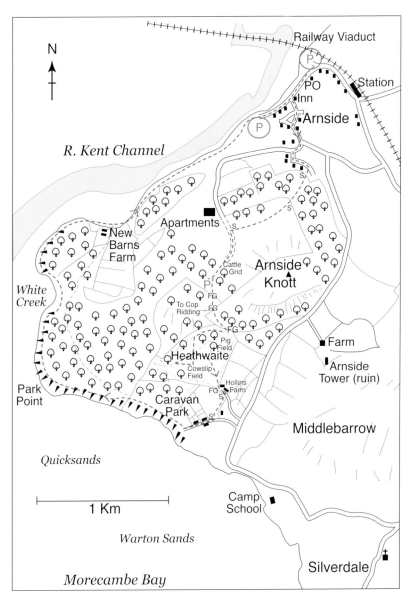

Map: use OS Outdoor Leisure (NS) 7, English Lakes SE Area
or OS Pathfinder 636, Grange over Sands

WALK 7 ◆ ARNSIDE

Distance 10 km / 6¼ miles
Time 3½–4½ hours

To get there turn off A6 at Milnthorpe, follow B5282 to Arnside. Park near the railway (SD455786) or on waterfront (SD458790). Walk up Silverdale Road, turn R along Redhills Road. After 120m go L along High Knott Road, then L after 150m, and a further 200m on take footpath on R. Footpath ascends through wood 400m to stile. Cross field ahead keeping wall on R to meet road. At road ascend L to NT car park and take track to L. Continue through two field gates to a third on R signed Heathwaite. Go R along footpath signed NT trail. After about 200m, still on trail, take L fork crossing main path into meadow. Continue in a loop to R to rejoin main path. Turn R along it to previous crossing place, from which descend through herb-rich meadow to field gate at bottom L corner. Go through gate down towards Hollins Farm. After next gate, over stile on R, take footpath across field towards Morecambe Bay. At road, go R through caravan park, footpath signed White Creek. At fork to clifftop path, either continue past other caravan sites to Arnside, or descend L to walk on clifftop or, if tide is out, along sands.

NB Tide flows very quickly, and quicksands abound.

An inexpensive NT leaflet with details of flora and fauna and nature trails is on sale at Arnside Post Office.

LOOK OUT FOR

Mar, Apr	Wild Daffodil, Wood Anemone, Primrose
May	Lily of Valley, False Oxlip, Early Purple Orchid
June	Herb Paris, Bloody Cranesbill, Spotted Orchid
July	Eyebright, Thyme, Rock-Rose, Agrimony
August	Centaury, Sweet Basil, Dropwort, Hemp Agrimony
September	Golden Rod, Burnet Saxifrage, Devil's Bit Scabious

Ferns include Hart's Tongue, Spleenwort, Wall Rue, Hard Fern, and in tufa forming on cliff just before you reach coastguard station, Maidenhair Fern (very rare in England).

Birds include Green Woodpecker, Blackcap, Willow Warbler, Long-Tailed Marsh, Great and Blue Tits and Jay; in autumn, visiting Fieldfares, Redwings and occasionally Waxwings strip berries from Holly, Rowan and Yew trees.

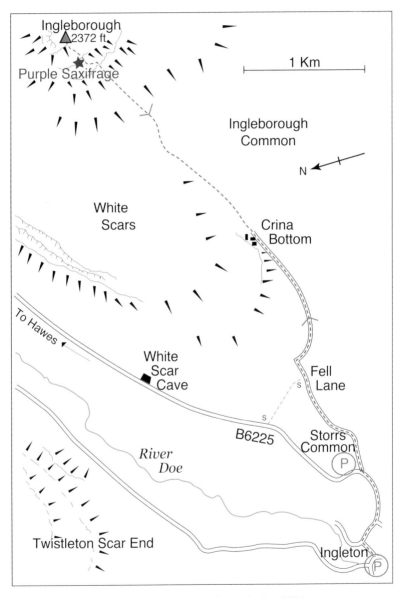

Map: use OS Outdoor Leisure Map (NS) 7, Yorkshire Dales S and W Areas
or (OS) 2, Yorkshire Dales West

WALK 8A ⬦ INGLEBOROUGH

Distance 11.5 km / 7½ miles
Time 4–4½ hours

Park at Ingleton car park (SD696732).
Walk up hill towards Hawes to Storrs
Common; limited car parking on
roadside (SD70132) shortens walk by
1km. Follow Fell Lane starting easterly
past Crina Bottom Farm then continue
by well-marked and partly engineered
track. At second escarpment look L at
crags, where early in the year Purple
Saxifrage can be seen within 4m of
path. Photograph, but do not pick or
move any of this very rare alpine plant.
From this point (SD739744), go on to
Ingleborough summit, 723m/2,372ft
for splendid views, and explore the
hut circles and boundary wall of the
Brigantian fort (see below). To return,
retrace outward path back to start.

LOOK OUT FOR

mid-March	Purple Saxifrage in flower
April	Purple Saxifrage, Whitlow Grass
May	Milkmaid, Tormentil
June	Mossy Saxifrage (near Purple Saxifrage), Wild Thyme
July	Heath Bedstraw, Silverweed
August	Devil's Bit Scabious, Harebell
September	Yarrow, Marsh Thistle

Ingleborough Hill Fort

The Roman subjugation of Britain began in 43 AD under Emperor Claudius. By 59 AD
Southern Britain, the Midlands and Wales were under Roman domination. The North of
England, under the control of the British Brigantian tribe and its leader Cartimandua, quickly
agreed to pay tribute to the Romans to keep the peace. Her consort and army commander
Venutius, outraged by this and her betrayal of Caractacus who had come to her for sanctuary,
broke away and set up a rebel army. He established a base at Stanwick near Scotch Corner
which eventually developed into a large fortified settlement. By 69 AD he had constructed a
wall, Ta Dyke, on a defensive scarp above Kettlewell, had set up a look-out fort at Gregory Hill
near Grassington and established a fort on top of Ingleborough (note hut circles and boundary
wall). But by 74 AD the Romans had defeated Venutius' army which completed the
subjugation of the Brigantes.

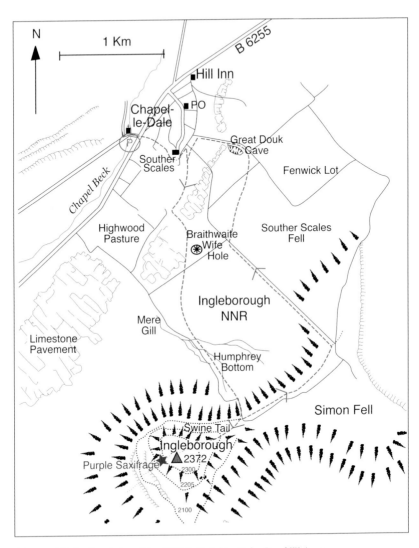

Map: use OS Outdoor Leisure Map (NS) 7, Yorkshire Dales S and W Areas
or (OS) 2, Yorkshire Dales West

WALK 8B ◆ INGLEBOROUGH

Distance 10 km / 6¹/₄ miles
Time 3¹/₂–4¹/₂ hours
Strenuous in places

Park opposite chapel in Chapel-le-Dale just off B6255 Ingleton–Hawes road (SD 737773). Walk back across B6225, over facing stile past Souther Scales Farm. Follow track L at first, below Souther Scales Scar via Braithwaite Wife Hole and Humphrey Bottom before the steep ascent up The Arks to Swine Tail. Here go R to summit at 723m/2,372 ft. To see Purple Saxifrage, leave summit cairn by Ingleton path at 240°. Just within second escarpment see *Saxifraga oppositifolia* close to R of path (as elsewhere on this contour). Do not pick or disturb this very rare alpine. Return by the same route to Swine Tail then contour R along flank of Simon Fell to steeply descending wall, which follow down through the National Nature Reserve and Souther Scales Fell back to start.

LOOK OUT FOR

Flowers as in Walk 8A, plus many other species in the gentler meadows towards the valley bottom. In spring the drumming mating call of the Snipe, caused by the vibration of its small lateral tail feathers during fast descents, is frequently heard, along with the bubbling calls of the Curlew and the 'peewit' of the Lapwing.

For most of the walk the Settle–Carlisle Railway and its famous Ribblehead Viaduct will be seen with Whernside to the left of it. Our route passes along the course of the famous Three Peaks Challenge, a 24-mile walk over Pen-y-Ghent, Whernside and Ingleborough, involving some 1,524m/5,000ft of ascents, to be completed within 12 hours.

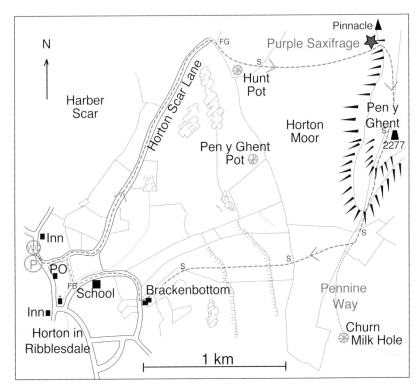

Map: use OS Outdoor Leisure Map (NS) 7, Yorkshire Dales S and W Areas
or (OS) 2, Yorkshire Dales West

WALK 9 ◆ PEN Y GHENT

Distance 9.5 km / 6 miles
Yime 4–4½ hours

On B6479 between Settle and Ribblehead, park at the Yorkshire Dales National Park car park in Horton-in-Ribblesdale (SD807725). Cross road opposite, go R. Just before the post office, take Horton Scar Lane on L for 2.5km. At gate, take footpath to R past Hunt Pot, over stile, then on engineered path to foot of Pen y Ghent escarpment. Where the path veers sharply R to ascend rake, cross slightly L towards the Pinnacle on the cliff face. Hereabouts in the frost-shattered scar, Purple Saxifrage grows. It is usually in full bloom during the first week of April, but may be seen in mid-March. From here the gentle uphill rake takes you to Pen y Ghent summit at 694m/2,277ft which affords spectacular views. Descend with a short scramble down the ridge to a stile on the R side. Here you leave the Pennine Way, on which you have walked all the way from Horton. Cross the stile and follow a clear path through limestone scars to Brackenbottom Farm. Turn R along road then first R over a footbridge and along a facing lane back to the start. To avoid rock scrambling, return from the Purple Saxifrage site on the same path back to Horton. The reverse of this walk is slightly easier.

Horton means Horse Town, where the monks of Jervaulx Abbey bred work- and war-horses, as they also did at Middleham, still a well-known horse-rearing area. It is an Anglian settlement with a Norman Church dating from about 1100. For most people, the Pen-y-Ghent Café in Horton is the start and finish of the classic Three Peaks Walk (see note to Walk 8B).

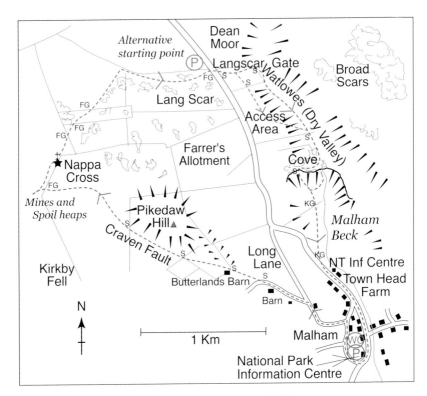

Map: use OS Outdoor Leisure (NS) 7, Yorkshire Dales S and W Areas
or (OS) 10, Yorkshire Dales South

WALK 10 ◆ MALHAM

Distance 9.5 km / 6 miles
Time 3¹/₂–4 hours

Park at Malham National Park Centre
(SD900627). Take walled lane behind
car park, then second lane on L, forking
L again to pass a series of field barns.
Immediately after a stream crossing
go R over a stile, pass R of Butterlands
Barn, then on up path below Henber
Side of Pikedaw Hill. Here the path
follows the Craven Fault: limestone
rocks and walls to R, gritstone rocks
and walls to L. Limestone outcrops
worth exploring. Continue NW along
path to fell wall. Disused lead, calamine
(a zinc ore) and copper mines can be
detected by spoil heaps hereabouts.
Through fell gate go R along bridleway
to road at Langscar Gate. Cross and
go ahead to two stiles leading into
Watlowes (Dry Valley), which follow
down to Cove (alternative route
through access area via stile in wall
to R approaching Watlowes). At cove,
look in grykes for Baneberry, etc.
Jacob's Ladder grows on cliffs to E.
Cross limestone pavement and follow
track back past NT information barn
to village and start.

LOOK OUT FOR

April	Milkmaid, Scurvy Grass, Mountain Pansy
May	Barren Strawberry, Marsh Marigold, Milkwort
June	Wild Thyme, Crosswort, Baneberry (in grykes)
July	Limestone Bedstraw, Salad Burnet, Wild Basil
August	Eyebright, Harebell, Orpine (cliff, Watlowes)
September	Devil's Bit Scabious, Cat's Ear, Marjoram
October	Maidenhair, Green Spleenwort, Hart's Tongue Fern

Birds include Wren, Meadow Pipit,
Carrion Crow, Wheatear, Curlew,
Black-headed Gull and Fieldfare
early and late in year.

Pikedaw Hill is an English Nature access area; free leaflets showing access points are available
at the Information Centres. A. R. Raistrick, *Malham and Malham Moor* (Dalesman, 1st edn
1947), chapters 5 and 8, gives a very informative background and commentary on this walk.

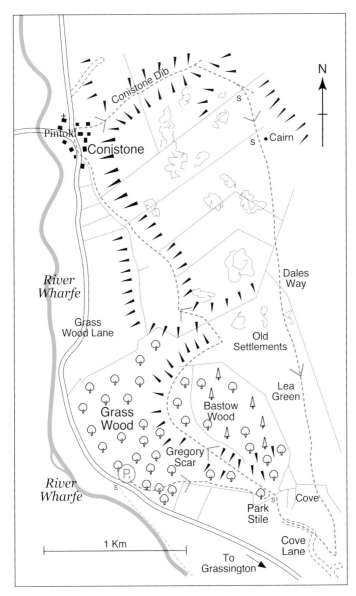

Map: use OS Outdoor Leisure (NS) 2, Yorkshire Dales S and W Areas
or (OS) 10, Yorkshire Dales South

WALK 11
GRASS WOOD & CONISTON DIB

Distance 13 km / 8 miles
Time 4–4¹/₂ hours

Park at old quarry on Grass Wood Lane
(SD985651). Follow footpath around
S edge of wood to Park Stile 995651.
Go L along public right of way past
Brigantian settlement (see note to
Walk 8) on L to finger post R at Bastow
Wood. Over stile at edge of wood go
straight on past a dew pond. At stile
over wall go L (keeping wall to R),
R at fork, then a clear path descends
to Conistone. At road go R for 200m,
turning R at Pinfold then R through
village green. Path climbs a narrow
gorge at first, then a wider valley. At
end of second field cross stile on R and
follow Dales Way (signed Grassington).
Follow this past Bronze and Iron Age
settlements and old lead mines. Just
before farm, footpath sharp R leads
down to Cove Lane. Follow to Cove
Lane and go through wood back to
start.

LOOK OUT FOR

March	Lesser Celandine, Whitlow Grass, Stinking Hellebore
April	Goldilock's Buttercup, Barren Strawberry, Primrose
May	Bird's Nest Orchid, Bird's Eye Primrose, Herb Paris
June	Valerian, Woodruff, Lily of the Valley
July	Spring Sandwort, Creeping Cinquefoil, Golden Rod
August	Marjoram, Creeping Bellflower, Wild Basil
September	Lady's Bedstraw, Devil's Bit Scabious, Figwort

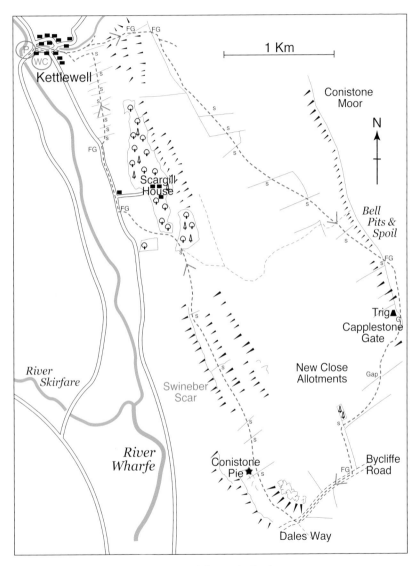

Maps: use OS Outdoor Leisure (NS) 10, Yorkshire Dales South
or (OS) 30, Yorkshire Dales North and Central

WALK 12 ◆ KETTLEWELL SOUTH

Distance 14 km / 9 miles
Time 4¹/₂–5¹/₂ hours

Park at National Park car park in
Kettlewell (SD968723). Walk past
Old Smithy, follow road L past
Maypole, bearing R after King's Head
Inn. Just before road bridge over stream
follow bridleway on R up to second
field gate after enclosed reservoir.
Through gate, cross fields to R
ascending gently through a series of
stiles up to field gate at moor edge.
Weave S through old bell pits and spoil
heaps to Capplestone Gate, then follow
Conistone Turf Road down to Bycliffe
Road; go R down to Dales Way. Turn R
past Scargill House (Bradford Diocesan
Retreat House) to road. At field gate
(SD975715) follow footpaths through
fields to Kettlewell and start.

A LOOK OUT FOR

April	Lesser Celandine, Milkmaid, Dove's Foot Cranesbill
May	Rue-Leaved Saxifrage, Sweet Cicely, Jack by the Hedge
June	Limestone Bedstraw, Salad Burnet, Rock-Rose
July	Cinquefoil, Tormentil, Eyebright
August	Bloody Cranesbill, Hedge Parsley, Brooklime
September	Harebell, Yarrow, Burnet Saxifrage

Birds include Lapwing, Curlew,
Oyster Catcher, Wheatear, Crow,
Swallow, Cuckoo, Skylark,
Meadow Pipit, Jackdaw, Magpie.

The Dales Way is a long-distance footpath, 81 miles in length, between Ilkley and Bowness-
on-Windermere. Its course is largely by riverside paths, but between Grassington and
Kettlewell it deviates from the meandering Wharfe to cross Lea Green, Conistone Old Pasture
and Swineber Scar for spectactular scenery, ancient settlements and field systems, with
occasional remains of its lead-mining heritage.

Kettlewell, from OE *cetel-wella*, stream in a narrow valley, or bubbling spring
O Brit *wharfe*, a winding river

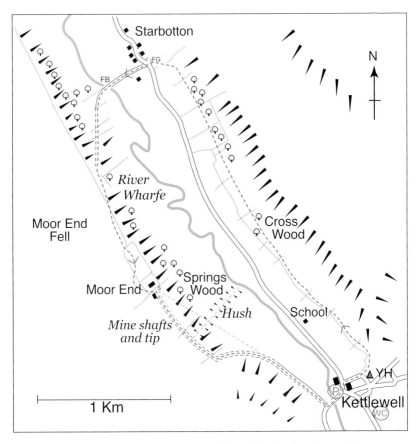

Map: use OS Outdoor Leisure (NS or OS) 30, Yorkshire Dales North and Central Areas

WALK 13 ◆ KETTLEWELL NORTH

Distance 8 km / 5 miles
Time 3–4 hours

Park at the National Park car park in Kettlewell (SD968723). Walk L over humpback bridge and up road to L of Bluebell Inn. Where road veers R past youth hostel, go straight ahead to a stile leading to an elevated path that skirts the pastures to the L. Continue on over many stiles to Starbotton. Cross straight over the B6160 and down lane to footbridge over River Wharfe. Take bridleway straight ahead signed Arncliffe, and continue through scar wood to open fell. From here to Moor End footpaths and bridleways have been substantially diverted, so most maps are now inaccurate. But follow guide posts to Moor End. From Moor End the farm track/bridleway descends back to Kettlewell's New Bridge and the start. An alternative field path is shown on the map.

LOOK OUT FOR

March	Primrose, Wood Anemone, Wood Sorrel
April	Sweet Cicely, Cowslip, Mountain Pansy
May	Scurvy Grass, Milkmaid, Bluebell
June	Barren Strawberry, Bird's Eye Primrose, Spotted Orchid, Butterwort
July	Eyebright, Crosswort, Lady's Bedstraw
August	Felwort, Creeping Bellflower, Spring Sandwort
September	Milkwort, Valerian, Melancholy Thistle

Interesting features to look out for on this walk include:

DRY STONE WALLS, mostly dating from the Enclosure Acts 1780–1820, but some dating from monastic times

MEDIEVAL GREEN LANES or DROVE ROADS developed by the monks of Fountains and Jervaulx Abbeys and the friars of Bolton Priory

HAY MEADOWS with FIELD BARNS serving two fields each

LYNCHETS or terraced fields established by the early Danish settlers

HUSHES and TAILINGS (spoil heaps) from lead-mining

MINERS' SMALLHOLDINGS, outlines on the valley flanks

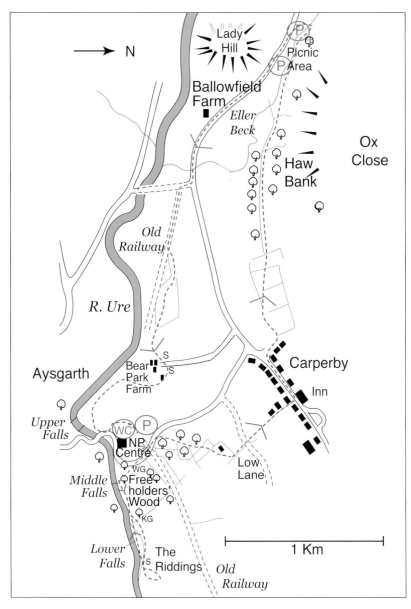

Map: use OS Outdoor Leisure (NS *or* OS) 30, Yorkshire Dales North and Central Areas

WALK 14 • CARPERBY & AYSGARTH FALLS

Distance 9 km / 5 1/2 miles
Time 3 1/2–4 1/2 hours or more

The walk starts at a picnic area beside the road between Askrigg and Carperby, 1km E of Woodhall (SD 988898). About 1km E along road past Ballowfield turn into lane on R for 100m then L on to disused railway line for 400m. Go L alongside a wall for 100m, then R across field to skirt Bear Park Farm and meet River Ure at Aysgarth Upper Falls. On to road, then take footpath immediately on L up to Aysgarth National Park Centre (toilets, café, information). Follow well-marked trail through Freeholders' Wood, dropping to view Middle and Lower Falls, riverside cliffs and pavement. Look in The Riddings for flowers (access courtesy of Yorkshire Dales National Park). Return by same route to road. Go R up road for 200m then take footpath on R to Carperby. Turn L. At W end of village, just past market cross on the village green, take footpath over fields, initially skirting football field, to descend down Haw Bank to start.

LOOK OUT FOR

Interesting diversity of plants at picnic area: especially Thrift, Orchids, Devil's Bit Scabious, Grass of Parnassus

In Freeholders' Wood, coppiced by National Park: Wood Anemone, Primrose, Columbine, St John's Wort, Wild and Barren Strawberry, Bluebell, Ramsons, Early Purple Orchid

In the wet flushes: Marsh Marigold, Marsh Valerian

By the riverside: Mountain Everlasting

In Riddings Field: wide range of interesting plants, including Burnt-Tip Orchid

Birds include Dippers, Sandpipers, Wagtails and Swallows, Nuthatch, Tree Creeper, Woodpeckers, Warblers and Finches, among many other species.

Askrigg from OE *aescric*, ash stream
Aysgarth from ON *eikiskaro*, gap with the oak wood
Carperby from OIr *cairpre*, a person; ON *by*, settlement
Riddings from OE *ryding*, clearing
Eller Beck from OE *elrebek*, alder stream

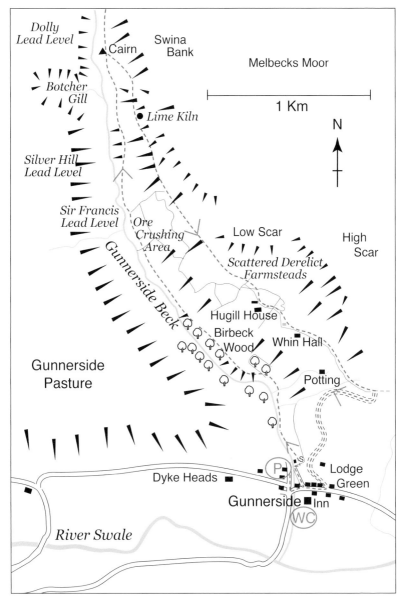

Map: use OS Outdoor Leisure (NS *or* OS) 30, Yorkshire Dales North and Central Areas

WALK 15 ◆ GUNNERSIDE

Distance 8 km / 5 miles
Time 3–3½ hours

Park in Gunnerside Village
(SD 951983). Walk up the narrow
lane on E of Gunnerside Gill opposite
The King's Head. After 150m footpath
starts up a few steps, then follow the gill
through woodland to reach the remains
of the Sir Francis Lead Mine. Follow
waymarks along valley bottom towards
the Bunton Mine. When opposite
Dolly Mine to W, at Cairn, take the
track that rakes gently upwards SE
passing the Barbara Mine, an old
limekiln, on the L and Hugill House
on the R. Farm track continues to a
fork. Take the R fork leading to tarmac
road that winds steeply down to the
village and starting point.

LOOK OUT FOR

Mar–Apr	Toothwort, Broomrape
May	Primrose, Wood Sorrel, Scurvy Grass
June	Sweet Cicely, Water Avens, Milkmaid
July	Marsh Valerian, Hoary Whitlow Grass, Sea Plantain
August	Sanicle, Spring Sandwort, Mountain Pansy
September	Meadowsweet, Foxglove, Milkwort

Spring Sandwort (*Minuartia verna*), known locally as Leadwort, is one of the first plants to colonise mineral-rich mine spoil.

This area is steeped in lead-mining history. For a good background, read R. Clough, *The Lead Smelting Mills of the Yorkshire Dales* (1962) and Thomas Armstrong, *Adam Brunskill* (Collins 1952), a very readable novel set in nineteenth-century Gunnerside.

Gunnerside is a corruption of 'Gunnar's saetr', from ON *saetr*, shieling (summer steading) and the name of its Danish founder, Gunnar. The village is still known locally by some as Gunnersett.

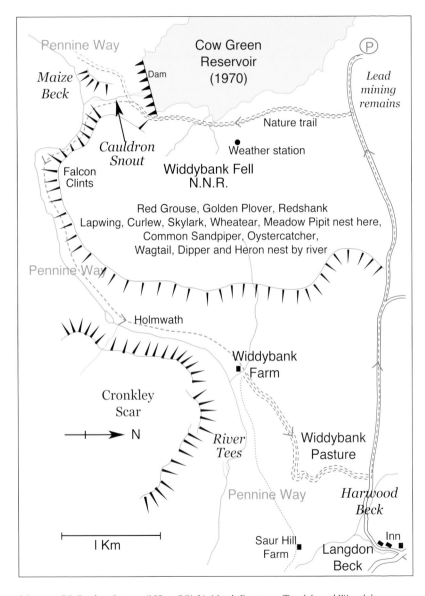

Map: use OS Outdoor Leisure (NS or OS) 31, North Pennines, Teesdale and Weardale

WALK 16
WIDDYBANK FELL, UPPER TEESDALE

Distance 13.5 km / 8¼ miles
Time 4–5 hours

To get there, follow the B6277 between
Middleton-in-Teesdale and Alston to
Langdon Beck (NY 853314), then take
Harwood Road on L, south at first
forking L after 2.5km to old lead-
mining area on shores of Cow Green
Reservoir, where there is a free car park
(NY 811309). Take waymarked nature
trail to Cauldron Snout. Descend past
cataracts and follow Pennine Way to
Widdybank Farm. Follow farm track to
Harwood Road turning L back to start.

Distance 10 km / 6¼ miles
Time 3½–4 hours

A shorter walk terminating at Falcon
Clints, whence return by the same
path. Look out for rare plants there,
including Holly Fern where whinsill
overlies limestone.

LOOK OUT FOR

Whitlow Grass, Thyme, Spring
Sandwort, Fairy Flax, Harebell,
Rock-Rose, Bird's Eye Primrose
and Mountain Pansy (purple here).

On the sugar limestone you will
see in season the rare Spring
Gentian, Alpine Bistort, Sea
Plantain and Mountain
Everlasting.

In wet flushes look out for
Bird's Eye Primrose, Butterwort
and Bog Asphodel.

In damp rocky areas, Yellow
Mountain Saxifrage and Knotted
Pearlwort.

Keen eyes will spot Moonwort
close to the track, especially near
the weather station.

A Nature Trail Guide Book is available at Cow Green, indicating what flowers to look out
for and where to find them.

WARNING
Cow Green at 503m/1,650ft can be very cold. Take warm clothing, water- and windproof.
Across the River Tees is an army firing range; you should be able to spot the warning flags.

TICKS & LYME DISEASE

The Lakes and Dales of Northern England are vast sheep-walks, often over-grazed because of indiscriminate 'headage' subsidies. Co-existing with the sheep are growing numbers of deer, particularly the ubiquitous Roe. The sheep, deer and other large animals are host to tiny blood-sucking ticks no more than 1.5mm/¹⁄₁₆in long.

Members of the spider family, they complete their larval and nymphal stages on small mammals such as wood mice and voles, then lurk in grasses, bracken and bushes until they can latch on to some passing prey, from which man is not excluded. They crawl unde-tectedly over the skin to some relatively tender spot then insert their barbed mouthpiece and, firmly anchored, draw blood without at first being felt. If left undisturbed, they gorge them selves to the size of a pea and then drop off, but long before then they are betrayed by the irritation this causes.

Tick, with an indication of its actual size

Removal is difficult because of the barbed mouthpart. The most satisfactory method is to smother the tick in petroleum jelly for about fifteen minutes then, with a sharp instrument such as the point of a penknife, prise it out. But care must be taken to remove all the head, or skin infec-tion can result. After removal, the skin should be wiped with antiseptic.

Barbed tick head, sketched from an electron microscope view

My more drastic treatment is to strike a match, blow out the flame, and apply the stick, still hot, to the tick. This has the double effect of making the tick release itself and cauterising the point of insertion.

However, just as the Anopheles mosquito can carry the malaria bacterium, ticks may carry a bacterium called *Borrelia burgdorferi* which can cause an infection called Lyme Disease. This starts as a rash that spreads outwards from the bite, enlarges nearby lymph glands and induces feverishness. Sufferers may feel very tired and suffer sundry aches and pains. Antibiotics effectively cure the condition, but in a few extreme cases facial paralysis, meningitis and abnormal skin sensations may occur.

It is important, therefore, when you are walking bare-legged or bare-armed or lying down to get a closer look at some small plant, to examine your clothing fairly often to check for infestation. When bathing, feel for tiny hard black spots on the legs and arms.

The disease is fairly common in the USA as well as in other countries worldwide. It was first diagnosed and named in Old Lyme, USA, in 1974, although it had been widespread in Europe since at least the turn of the century.

FURTHER READING

Back, P., *The Illustrated Herbal* (Hamlyn, 1987)

Blamey, M. and C. Grey-Wilson, *Illustrated Flora of Britain and Northern Europe* (Hodder & Stoughton, 1994)

Blunt, W., *The Complete Naturalist*, (Collins, 1971)

Bown, D., *RHS Encyclopaedia of Herbs* (Dorling Kindersely, 1995)

Ceres, *The Healing Power of Herbal Teas* (Thorsons, 1984)

Chevallier, A., *Encyclopaedia of Medicinal Plants* (Dorling Kindersley, 1996)

Coombes, A. J., *Dictionary of Plant Names* (Collingridge, 1985)

Culpeper, N., *Culpeper's Complete Herbal* (1699; reprint Wordsworth, 1995))

de Gex., J., *A Medieval Herbal* (Pavilion, 1995)

Dorfler, H. P. and G. Roselt, *Dictionary of Healing Plants* (Blandford, 1989)

Duncan, J. E. and R. W. Robson, *Pennine Flowers* (Dalesman, 1977)

Clapham, A. R., ed., *Upper Teesdale* (Collins, 1978)

Fitter, R. A. and M. Blamey, *Wild Flowers of Britain and Northern Europe* (Collins, 1974)

Gerard, J., *Gerard's Herbal* (reprint Senate, 1994)

Gilmour, J. and M. Walters, *Wild Flowers* (Collins New Naturalist Series, 1954)

Gledhill, D., *The Names of Plants* (Cambridge University Press, 2002)

Gordon, L., *A Country Herbal* (Webb & Bowes, 1980)

Grieve, M., *A Modern Herbal* (Tiger, 1931)

Grigson, G., *The Englishman's Flora* (Phoenix House, 1958)

Grigson, G., *Dictionary of English Plant Names* (Lane, 1973)

Grounds, R., *Ferns* (Readers' Union, 1975)

Halliday, G, *A Flora of Cumbria* (Lancaster University, 1997)

Launert, E., *Edible Medicinal Plants of Britain and Northern Europe* (Country Life, 1981)

Louseley, J. E., *Wild Flowers of Chalk and Limestone* (Collins New Naturalist Series, 1950)

Mabey, R., *Flora Britannica* (Sinclair Stevenson, 1996)

McClintock, D. and R. S. R. Fitter, *Pocket Guide to Wild Flowers* (Collins, 1956)

Grieve, M., *A Modern Herbal* (Cape, 1931)

Merryweather, J. and M. Hill, *The Fern Guide* (Field Studies Council, 1992)

Millward, D., *A Flora of Wensleydale* (Yoredale Nature Society, 1988)

Phillips, R., *Wild Flowers of Britain* (Ward Lock, 1977)

Press, B., *Green Guide: Herbs* (New Holland, 1994)

Raistrick, A. and J. L. Illingworth, *The Face of N.W. Yorkshire* (Dalesman, 1949)

Raven, J. and M. Walters, *Mountain Flowers* (Collins New Naturalist Series, 1956)

Sanecki, K. N., *Complete Book of Herbs* (Macdonald, 1974)

Stearn, W. T., *Botanical Latin* (David & Charles, 1966)

Summerhayes, V. S., *Wild Orchids of Britain* (Collins New Naturalist Series, 1951)

Vickery, R., *A Dictionary of Plant Lore* (Oxford University Press, 1995)

Watts, W. M., *A School Flora* (Longmans, 1905)

INDEX OF PLANT NAMES